Journal of the

INDIAN WARS

Volume One, No. 4

Savas Publishing Company

202 First Street SE, Suite 103A, Mason City, IA 50401

Subscription and Publishing Information

Journal of the Indian Wars (*JIW*) is published quarterly by Savas Publishing Company, 202 First Street SE, Suite 103A, Mason City, IA 50401. Publisher: Theodore P. Savas. (515) 421-7135 (voice); (515)-421-8370 (fax); e-mail: cwbooks@mach3ww.com. Our online military history catalog of original books is found at www.savaspublishing.com.

SUBSCRIPTIONS to *JIW* are available at $29.95/yr. (four books); Canada and overseas is $39.95/yr. Write to: Savas Publishing Company, *JIW* Subscriptions, 202 First Street SE, Suite 103A, Mason City, IA 50401. Check, MO, MC or V accepted. Phone, fax or e-mail orders welcome. All subscriptions begin with the current issue unless otherwise specified.

DISTRIBUTION in North America is handled by Peter Rossi at Stackpole Books, 5067 Ritter Road, Mechanicsburg, PA 17055-6921. 800-732-3669 (voice); 717-976-0412 (fax); E-mail: prossi@stackpolebooks.com. European distribution is through Greenhill Books, Park House, 1 Russell Gardens, London NW11 9NN, England; E-mail: LionelLeventhal@compuserve.com; Back issues of *JIW* are available through Stackpole Books or your local bookseller. Retail price is $11.95 plus shipping ($4.00 for the first book and $1.00 for each additional book). Check, money order, MC/V, AE, or D are accepted. Contact Stackpole Books for quantity discounts.

MANUSCRIPTS, REVIEWS, AND NEWS SUBMISSIONS are welcome. For guidelines, consult our web site (www.savaspublishing.com), or send a self-addressed stamped envelope to Michael A. Hughes, Editor, *Journal of the Indian Wars*, 834 East Sixth Street, Box E, Ada, OK 74820. Proposals for articles (recommended) should include a brief description of your topic, a list of primary sources, and estimate of completion date. Manuscripts should be accompanied by a 3.5" disk with copies in both WordPerfect 6.1 (or lower) and Rich Text (RTF) formats. Persons interested in reviewing books should send a description of their qualifications, areas of expertise, and desired titles and topics. News submissions should include a brief abstracted version of any information. Submitted news may be posted on our web site at our discretion. Enclose a SASE if requesting a reply and include your e-mail and fax number. Publications (which may include page proofs) and videos for potential review should be sent to the managing editor.

Savas Publishing Company expressly disclaims all responsibility for statements, whether of opinion or fact, contained herein.

JIW is published with the cooperation of Jerry Russell and the Order of the Indian Wars. Without Jerry's non-too-gentle proddings and earnest supplications, it would not have come to fruition. For more information, please write to OIW, P.O. Box 7401, Little Rock AR 72217.

Savas Publishing Company

Publisher
Theodore P. Savas

Editorial Assistants: Patrick A. Bowmaster, William Haley
Graphics: James Zach
Marketing: Carol A. Savas
Indexing: Lee W. Merideth

Journal of the Indian Wars

Managing Editor: Michael A. Hughes
Associate Editors: Patrick A. Bowmaster, Rod Thomas,
Phil Konstantin, and Eril B. Hughes
Book Review Editor: Patrick Jung
Advertising/Circulation: Carol A. Savas
Editorial Consultants: Brian Pohanka,
Jerry Keenan, Neil Mangum, Jerry Russell, and Ted Alexander

Civil War Regiments Journal

Managing Editor: Theodore P. Savas

Assistant Editors: Lee Merideth, William Haley
Circulation/Advertising: Carol Savas
Book Review Editor: Archie McDonald

Cover Image:
"White Horse Battles the Delawares"
Courtesy of the Colorado Historical Society

Contributors

Jeff Broome is a professor of philosophy at Arapaho Community College in Colorado. Dr. Broome has written articles for at least four Indian wars publications as a result of his lifelong interest in the conflicts. He is currently working on a manuscript on the 1867 "Kidder Massacre."

Richard S. Grimes is a professor of history at West Virginia University. Dr. Grimes' current article in *JIW* is one of many articles and papers he has produced on Western Indian military societies.

Michael Hughes is the managing editor of *Journal of the Indian Wars* and an instructor in art history, humanities, and history at Oklahoma East Central University. He also leads a variety of art, archaeology, and history tours.

Kerry Oman is a doctoral student in history at Southern Methodist University in Dallas, Texas. He was formerly a graduate student at Brigham Young University, where he did research with the legendary Walter Camp Indian wars papers.

Gary Zeller is a graduate student at the University of Arkansas-Fayetteville, and will finalize his dissertation on African Creeks in the Civil War this summer. Gary has been an interim instructor at the University of Arkansas and at Sam Houston University and, is now seeking a permanent position teaching U.S. history.

Columnists this issue include associate editors Patrick A. Bowmaster and Phil Konstantin.

Journal of the
INDIAN WARS

Table of Contents

continued

Table of Contents (continued)

FOREWORD

Theodore P. Savas

This issue of *Journal of the Indian Wars* is very special. Volume One, No. 4 is the last issue of the first full year of publication. There were a few nay sayers out there on the Great Plains bellowing that we were attempting the impossible, but by and large prepublication support for the *JIW* concept was broad and deep.

The forever-controversial George Custer seemed a logical subject for the inaugural issue, and "Custer at the Washita and Little Bighorn" became reality last summer. Everyone working with this project held their collective breath, waiting to see how it would be judged. When subscriptions and letters of encouragement and praise began pouring in, we exhaled sighs of relief, lifted a pint, and returned to work.

We crawled out on a rather thin limb with the second issue. We knew we could not go wrong with Custer. But how would our readers react to articles on topics largely ignored by historians—and, as one reader gently chided us upon learning of the subject matter in advance of publication, "about actions on the wrong side of the Mississippi River?" To our utter delight, "Battles and Leaders East of the Mississippi" generated twice as much positive mail, calls, and subscriptions than the premiere issue. "I did not know if you folks were for real," wrote a new subscriber who had purchased the Custer issue from a bookstore and had just picked up the second issue. "Now, I know you are. Here is my check for a subscription."

The American Civil War and the Indian wars have many connections, but the experiences of Indians during the war have been overlooked by almost everyone writing on the former subject. Our next issue took a slightly different perspective by widely examining how the war impacted the individual Indians who served both North and South, as well as Western Indian nations, which were largely decimated by the conflict. Like the pair of issues preceding it, "The Indian Wars' Civil War" generated significant interest and enthusiasm. This brings us to the last issue of our first year.

Graduate student Gary Zeller opens *Famous Fighting Units* with "First to Fight for Freedom: African Creek Soldiers Enter the Civil War." It is "generally agreed," he writes, "that the first black Americans to fight in the Civil War were freemen and escaped slaves of African origin," and the first to battle for emancipation were the soldiers of the 54th Massachusetts, made famous by the movie *Glory*. (Students of the war know that the 1st Kansas Colored Infantry faced combat nine months before the 54th faced action). "While neither conclusion is an intentional lie," explains Zeller, "neither is true": What is neither generally agreed upon or even suspected "is that most of the first men of color to fight for freedom were still in bondage and that some of them were as much American Indian as African by birth."

Managing Editor Michael A. Hughes continues (and concludes) his encyclopedic examination of the experiences of Indian cultures in "Nations Asunder, Part II: Reservation and Eastern Indians During the American Civil War." The overshadowing sweep of the titanic struggle that ripped apart America obscured the hardships and suffering endured by most Indian nations. Hughes sheds considerable light on their plight by adding a few more brush strokes to the canvas that is our history and ultimately, our legacy.

"Modern Spartans on the Great Plains: The Ascent of the Cheyenne Dog Soldiers, 1838-1869," by Richard S. Grimes, sets forth in fascinating detail the origins of this militant group of warriors and their response to what they viewed as a national crisis (i.,e., the encroachment of white settlers). The Dog Soldiers, associated with famous warriors like Roman Nose, among others, "transcended their original responsibility and duty as a soldier society and rose to a position of military and political dominance among the Cheyenne people."

The fight at Beecher Island is generally known to readers of the Indian wars, but rarely has it been presented so adeptly as in Kelly Oman's "Island Besieged: Forsyth's Scouts at the Battle of Beecher Island." Oman develops the background of this famous unit, explains the complicated events leading up to the battle, and calls attention to the human drama and suffering (on both sides) of the nine-day affair. Only quick thinking and unsurpassed bravery spared Forsyth and his small band from experiencing their own Little Bighorn eight years before Custer.

This issue concludes with an wide-ranging interview (conducted by Jeff Broome, a professor at Arapahoe Community College in Colorado and author of numerous articles) of John H. Monnett, the author of a number of Indian wars-related books and articles.

This edition also features two new columns. "Konstantin's Quarter," by Phil Konstantin, will be a regular offering on what was happening in American Indian History. Phil runs one of the finest websites with the best available links to   Indian wars' research. "From the Front," by associate editor Patrick Bowmaster, will present our readers with a interesting information on a wide variety of topics of general interest. Pat's column is about a celebrated—and disgraced—Buffalo soldier who won the Medal of Honor. "The First Congressional Medal of Honor for a Buffalo Soldier" is a life and times exposé of Emanuel Stance, who earned plaudits for his actions against Indians and, on five different occasions, "lost his non-commissioned officer rank and was reduced to being a private for failure to perform his duty." His ultimate fate was even more unkind.

Once again, we thank you for your continued support, encouragement, and contributions as we struggle forth with this labor of love.

AFRICAN CREEK SOLDIERS
Enter the Civil War

Gary Zeller

N apoleon Bonaparte is alleged to have said that "history is a lie generally agreed upon." In the case of the American Civil War, there is occasionally some truth to the observation. For example, it is "generally agreed" that the first black Americans to fight in the Civil War were freemen and escaped slaves of African origin. It is also "generally agreed" that the first blacks to fight for emancipation were the soldiers of the Fifty-fourth Massachusetts Infantry made famous by the movie *Glory* (though students of the war know that the First Kansas Colored Infantry Regiment faced combat nine months before the Fifty-fourth faced battle). While neither conclusion is an intentional lie, neither is true. What is neither generally agreed upon or even suspected is that most of the first men of color to fight for freedom were still in bondage and that some of them were as much American Indian as African by birth.

By the fall of 1861, slaves and freemen of the Creek (Muskogee) Indian nation had already taken up arms to prevent losing what degree of liberty they already possessed. Throughout the winter of that year, they fought side by side with their Creek and Seminole allies on an exodus from the Indian Territory to what would become full freedom in Kansas. Later, as members of the tri-racial First Indian Home Guard Regiment, "African Creeks" would be the first black soldiers officially mustered in the Federal Army, the first to participate in combat in a regiment during the Civil War, and the first to fight in a major battle of the war. Others would enlist in the First and Second Kansas Colored

Regiments, so many that they would contribute a company of recruits for each unit. By war's end, the African Creek community may have supplied more Union soldiers per capita than any other population in America. Through four full years of conflict, they left the security of their homes and farms, or those of their Indian masters, for the battlefields of the Indian Territory, Arkansas, and Missouri in their struggle for freedom.[1] Yet, the experience of the African Creeks who fought in the Trans-Mississippi theater of the conflict remains one of the most neglected topics in Civil War history.

African Creeks were drawn into the American Civil War as a result of a civil conflict within the Creek [Muskogee] Nation. The sectional split between North and South over slavery translated into a rift among the Creeks that had its own unique cultural and political origins. Despite this, African Creek slaves and freemen early on found themselves at the center of the conflict within the tribe.[2]

As the secession crisis of the United States deepened in the early months of 1861, Southern politicians and pro-Confederate former officials from the U.S. Indian Office tried to convince the Creeks and nations of the [Oklahoma] Indian Territory to side with the Confederacy. Having for many years played a major role in the social, cultural, and economic life of the Indian Nation, African Creek slaves and free blacks had enjoyed a degree of freedom unmatched in any of the slave states. This may have been, in part, because some had a degree of Creek as well as African parentage. This experience of independence would serve them well at crucial times during the impending war. Pro-Southern Creeks and white slave holders in neighboring states looked at the scant supervision of the nearly two thousand African Creeks—including as many as three hundred free blacks—as a threat to the slave system. Pro-Confederate, pro-Southern factions within the tribe put pressure upon the Creek Council to end any degree of freedom for the African Creeks.

The Creek Council, in a first move towards alliance with the Confederacy, enacted a harsh series of laws designed to bring the African Creeks under closer control. The new laws took effect in March of 1861 and included provisions that would confine slaves to their master's lands, institute a pass and patrol system, and forbid slaves to own livestock or other property or hire out their labor for their own profit. Even worse, the new laws instructed all free African Creeks to reenter slavery by selecting a master. If they did not do so by March 10, 1861, they were to be sold to the highest bidder at government auction. Free blacks were also told they must dispose of all their property before returning to slavery. Tribal officers were appointed to oversee the free blacks' return to slavery, and the Creek Lighthorse, the tribal law enforcement body, was given authority to enforce the new code.[3]

The African Creeks were disturbed by these new laws. But in the early months of 1861, there appeared to be little they could do to reverse the course of events. The African Creeks were further disheartened when the leaders of the Lower Creek faction signed a treaty with the Confederacy in July of 1861 and recruited two Creek Confederate regiments. A coalition of pro-Southern Creek chiefs, joined by wealthy part-white, Lower Creek faction slave holders, now had power to enforce the new anti-freedom laws and to control the Creek tribe's future.[4]

The African Creeks were not the only persons within the Creek nation who were unsettled by the alliance with the Confederacy. The Upper Creek faction leaders, who had counseled neutrality in the "white man's war," were driven into active opposition against the tribal government after the Lower Creek leaders secured the Creek Council's approval of the Confederate Treaty. At a meeting held on August 5, Opothleyahola, along with other Upper Creek leaders, repudiated the terms of the new treaty. The insurgents declared the office of principal chief vacant and elected Oktarharsars Harjo (or Sands) their new tribal chief.

At first, the so-called Loyal Creeks, mostly from the Upper Creek towns, merely separated themselves from the pro-Southern faction and gathered in a camp on Opothleyahola's plantation. They hoped to remain unmolested there in their neutrality. The chances of maintaining that position while surrounded by Confederate regiments mustered for war were slim.[5]

On August 15, Opothleyahola and Sands wrote to ask President Abraham Lincoln for help:

> Now I write the President, Our Great Father who removed us to our present homes and made a treaty, and you said that in our new homes we should be defended from all interference from any person and that no white people in the whole world would ever molest us. . . . But now the wolf has come. Men who are strangers tread our soil. Our children are frightened and the mothers cannot sleep for fear. This is our situation now. When we made our treaty at Washington . . . we believed you. Then our Great Father was strong. Now White people are trying to take our people away to fight against us and you. I am alive. I well remember the treaty. My ears are open and my memory is good.[6]

Creek Chief Opothlayohola

Smithsonian Institution, National Anthropological Archives

The African Creek memory was good also. The slaves could recall that the traditionalist Opothleyahola had in earlier years ordered African Creeks whipped, not for disobedience but for accepting Christianity. Yet now the chief reached out to forge an alliance with the blacks in the Creek and Seminole Nations. Opothleyahola sent agents into the slave settlements and free black enclaves throughout the two Indian nations bearing promises of freedom to all African Muskogees who joined the "Loyal" [i.e., pro-Union] Creeks. Opothleyahola, in his new role as emancipator, found willing allies in the African Creeks. Faced with a choice between complete slavery and some degree of freedom, they needed little persuasion. They left their stores and blacksmith shops filled with merchandise and tools, their farms with apple trees laden with ripening fruit, and their corn cribs full from the harvest. They abandoned ranches stocked with fodder and hay and brought what livestock they could. Some deserted the farms and plantations of their masters, an occurrence that would be repeated throughout the slave states and territories in the coming years of struggle. Upper Creek masters provided their slaves and former slaves with wagons, horses, and provisions for sustenance and weapons for protection so that together they might make an exodus towards freedom. Together they sought refuge in Opothleyahola's camp at the mouth of the Deep Fork of the Canadian River, in the western part of Creek territory.[7]

An estimated 200-300 African Creeks and African Seminoles and 3,500 Creek Indian citizens gathered at Opothleyahola's and other camps between August and November of 1861. The majority of the African Creeks came from the Upper Creek faction country in the southern and western parts of the Muskogee Nation. Others came from farther away, from the Arkansas border district and from the area around the Creek Agency and Tullahassee Mission in the eastern and northern parts of the nation.[8]

The story of Simon Brown suggests how worsening conditions drove some African Creeks into active resistance to slavery and alliance with Opothleyahola. Brown was a slave of Hannah Brown, who lived near Tullahassee Mission, near the fork of the Verdigris and Arkansas rivers at the northeastern edge of Creek country. Although Simon Brown was a slave, in accordance with the relaxed Creek attitude toward slavery he had been permitted before the war to work for wages for the Robertson family, the missionaries at Tullahassee. Brown regularly made trips on errands for the Robertsons, frequently journeying alone as he did so.[9] In July of 1861, Simon drove the wagon that carried the Robertsons into forced exile out of the Creek Nation for the duration of the war.[10] We don't know what went through Simon's mind as he made his way home, but in November the "trusted slave" fled the increasingly restrictive and oppressive atmosphere and took his family to Opothleyahola's camp. Brown would later explain that his actions were the result of "atrocities committed against Negroes by rebel troops."[11]

As well as slaves like Brown, free African Creeks also fled to Opothlayohola. The provision in the new law code that required them to sell their property and return to slavery prompted many freemen to leave behind their lives of relative prosperity. Billy Hawkins, a free African Creek preacher from the Post Oak community, twelve miles west of the Creek Agency and just south of the Arkansas River, was another such refugee. Before the new laws were passed, Hawkins had regularly preached before mixed congregations at the Post Oak Baptist church. He had been able to travel freely to other churches or to camp meetings in the nation. Hawkins had a thriving farming and ranching operation at his place in Post Oak, where he owned eleven horses, five mules, two yokes of oxen, fifty-eight cattle and a hundred and forty hogs. In September of 1861 he gave up his prosperity and fled to Opothleyahola's camp for safety. This, he explained, was because he had "preached for the [United States] government" instead of remaining silent about his opposition to the Confederacy.[12]

Gilbert Lewis, a slave of Kendell Lewis, lived in "the Point," a peninsula of land between the Verdigris and Arkansas rivers, on the northeastern edge of Creek country. He and his family left their home late in the fall and journeyed the entire breadth of the troubled Creek Nation to reach the Loyal Creek camp. The country traversed bristled with armed men—Creeks, Choctaws, Seminoles, Chickasaws, Cherokees, and Texans, all sympathetic to the Confederacy. Yet, Lewis still chanced the journey because "[Creek Confederate Col. D. N.] McIntosh would not allow the Negroes to remain at their homes in possession of their property."[13]

For a variety of compelling reasons, many African Creeks—whether slave or free—made alliance with Opothleyahola. Some sought merely to expand the limited degree of personal freedom previously experienced even among some African Creeks. Others were motivated by the promise of full emancipation—a year before Abraham Lincoln announced his limited proclamation of emancipation for slaves in Confederate territory. Whatever their aim, some three hundred African Creeks actively resisted their enslavement in the most convincing way possible: like Gilbert Lewis, they spoke with their feet, abandoning their master's fields; like Billy Hawkins, they spoke with their voices, preaching from pulpits. Ultimately they took up arms, becoming the first black community in America to organize armed resistance to the Confederacy.[14]

Colonel (later General)
Douglas C. Cooper

Generals in Gray

As the African Creeks made their exodus, aggressive Creek Confederates like Daniel N. McIntosh and James S. Smith, were eager to strike at Opothleyahola and his followers. They had taken a hard line immediately after the Loyal Creeks' repudiation of the Confederate treaty and were intent on "mak[ing] them feel our law." Others, including former Choctaw agent and now Confederate commander of the Indian District, Col. Douglas C. Cooper, initially counseled patience as long as there were no armed demonstrations against Confederate government. Such restraint became increasingly difficult to maintain as Confederate Creeks became increasingly worried that Opothleyahola and his followers would join with Kansas "jayhawkers" and move against them. Armed bands of Kansans had begun raiding south into Indian Territory, and the abolitionist Kansas senator James H. Lane loudly and publicly proclaimed the need for Union forces to strike into the Indian Territory and blaze a trail into Texas.[15]

In the end, however, the principal reason that a combined force of Confederate Indians and Texans attacked the Loyal Creeks was their alarm and anger over the number of runaway slaves fleeing to Opothleyahola. As early as September 11, Colonel McIntosh, the commander of the First Confederate Creek Regiment, voiced his concern to John Drew, commander of a Confederate Cherokee regiment. "Negroes are fleeing to him [Opothleyahola] from all quarters—not less than 150 have left within the last three days," complained McIntosh. "This state of affairs cannot long exist here without seriously effecting [sic] your country. Therefore, [they] should be put down immediately."[16]

As Confederate hostility to their people grew, Opothleyohola and the "Loyal" chiefs rebuffed further entreaties for negotiations, insisting that their intentions were peaceful. In the first week of October, Opothleyahola received a message from Confederate Indian commissioner Albert Pike offering amnesty for all Creeks under arms against the Confederate States and the lawful authorities of the Creek Nation. The offer also contained the proviso that all fugitive slaves must be surrendered.[17] When the Loyal Creeks rejected the offer, Moty Kanard and Echo Harjo wrote to Cherokee leader John Ross, "Again they are causing our Negroes to run to them daily, greatly to the injury of many of our best citizens. These and other considerations make it necessary for them to be put down at all costs. Therefore as soon as we are reinforced, which we daily expect, we shall proceed without further delay and put an end to the affair."[18]

A week after the complaints to Ross, an Arkansas border newspaper reported that more than six hundred fugitive slaves from all the tribes in the Indian Territory and neighboring states had fled to the protection of Opothleyahola. The journalist disparagingly referred to the Creek leader as "'Old Gouge,' the insurgent chief," and said that help was on the way in the form of "a regiment of Texas troops." The regiment was due to arrive at the chief's farm in a few days. The white Arkansans who published the story were probably more relieved at the news than the Creek Confederates. Though the Texans were supposed to be their allies, the Confederate Creeks knew that the Texans on the way to save them had a reputation for dealing brutally with Indians as well as fugitive slaves.

Meanwhile, a Confederate Creek scouting report informed Colonel McIntosh that a party of Opothleyahola's followers that included "a large lot of Negroes" had crossed the Deep Fork river and were moving west and to the north. McIntosh and the other Indian officers decided it was time to act swiftly. They told Colonel Cooper that they intended to move against Opothleyahola and his party and that "all free Negroes found with Hopothleyohola's [sic] party and taken during the expedition shall be sold as slaves for the benefit of the Nation. All slaves that have joined (them) shall be sold also except in cases where the owner belongs to our party and is a member in this expedition. All slaves taken in this expedition who have runaway from their owners who are resident of another nation shall be dealt with according to Creek Law."[19]

Cooper still advised a negotiated settlement. But in preparation for a possible clash, and resulting seizure of property, Cooper notified the Creeks that slaves and goods captured during the expedition would be turned over to the Confederacy. Cooper also informed their officers that as he was now commander of all Confederate forces in the Indian Territory, all military operations within its boundaries would be under his direction.[20]

Cooper's expedition moved against the Loyal Muskogees on November 4. When they arrived the following day at the Loyal Muskogee main camp, located at the Big Bend of the Deep Fork, they found it abandoned. The Loyal Creeks, alerted of preparations for an attack, had broken camp and were headed north. Although the initial route of the Loyal Creeks is a subject of historical controversy, they were evidently headed toward Kansas. The Confederates pursued them, and the Loyal Creeks, protecting the women and children as best they could, fought the first three battles of the Civil War in the Indian Territory.[21]

African Creeks and African Seminoles participated in the battles of Round Mountain on November 19, Chusto Talasah (Bird Creek) on December 8, and Chustenahlah (Caving Banks) on December 26. Between fifty and one hundred men of African descent were under arms in the battles. Following their defeat at Round Mountain, some of the Texans grumbled about having to fight African Creeks at the battle. A Confederate Cherokee scouting party confronted a group of armed African Creeks and Creek Indians on December 5, just before the battle at Chusto Talasah. When the Cherokee scouts identified themselves as "soldiers of the South," one of the blacks "reprimed his gun," then "spoke back impudently" before continuing on. The Confederates, outnumbered and outgunned, decided to withdraw rather than confront the African and Creek allies.

The first two actions (Round Mountain and Chusto Talasah) had been holding actions, albeit successful ones, and the Loyal Creeks were able to continue toward Kansas. However, at the Battle of Chustenahlah, fought north of Tulsey Town (present-day Tulsa) on December 26, the Confederate pursuers finally overwhelmed the Loyal Creeks. During the fight on Hominy Creek, Confederates killed an undetermined number of armed men—Confederate reports said 250, surely a wild exaggeration—and captured 160 women and children as well as the bulk of the livestock and provisions carried by the refugees. The Confederates also captured twenty African Creeks and Seminoles, most of them women and children. The surviving refugees, without food, clothing, shelter, or even shoes, staggered on to Kansas through a freezing winter storm. They suffered horribly from hunger and cold along the way, and many died of exposure. Thirty-five hundred Creek refugees along with approximately two thousand more Indians from other tribes survived and eventually reached their destination.[22]

The Loyal refugees reached Kansas during the first weeks in January in a wretched condition. Frostbite, hunger, and disease were rampant. One of the first doctors on the scene, U.S. Army Surgeon A. B. Campbell, reported performing over one hundred amputations in a few days. Campbell also said pneumonia, consumption, and other "inflammatory diseases of the chest, throat and eyes" associated with exposure were common among the refugees. Few had provisions for even the rudest of shelters and instead slept on the frozen ground with piles of prairie grass for bedding. Shoes were unknown, and food and clothing were in short supply. Refugees wandered the camps, naked in the freezing temperatures, searching for food and clothing for themselves and their families. At the direction of Gen. David A. Hunter, the commander of the District of Kansas, the U.S. Army fed the refugees from January through February 15, 1862. Hunter had been following developments in the Indian Territory with great interest and had even tried to raise a regiment of Kansas Indians to aid the Loyal Creeks during the fall of 1861. He doubled his efforts after the refugees appeared in Kansas.[23]

The Indian Office took over the job of providing subsistence for the refugees on February 15. The Southern Superintendent for Indian Affairs, William S. Coffin, worked with scant resources and juggled the books to come up with a daily ration that cost thirty cents per refugee per day. Coffee and sugar were cut from the provision in order to halve the cost. Refugees were allowed only one pound of flour apiece weekly. Not only were the rations meager, but the food itself was barely fit to eat. Most of the flour was wet and spoiled. Indian Office officials tried to give the refugees bacon that had been rejected by the Army at Ft. Leavenworth, Kansas, as fit only for providing grease for making soap. The refugees, even in their starving condition, refused the condemned bacon, claiming it was not "fit for a dog to eat." For shelter, the Army provided discarded army tents and unfitted canvas.

The Indian Office did not provide any subsistence for the slaves among the refugees. Instead, their Indian masters and patrons were supposed to provide for them. However, it was often the African Creeks who looked out for the Indians. The Indian Office agents in charge of dispensing the subsistence had to be to accompanied by interpreters, who were often African Creeks. The interpreters helped compile lists of refugees and their families for the issuing agents and made sure that that the subsistence was fairly distributed. Black interpreters were also in demand to help provide medical services. A. V. Coffin, the Indian Office's doctor for the refugees, said it was necessary to prepare medicines and then leave them with the interpreters to administer, since the Indians would trust no one else to dispense them. Coffin also attempted to use his interpreters to instruct the Indians in "sanitary and healthful practices." He had more luck persuading the African Creeks to accept practices like smallpox vaccinations than he did the Indians, as mortality figures aptly demonstrate.[24]

As the weather warmed during the spring of 1862, over one thousand Indian pony carcasses littering the banks of the Verdigris River near the camps began to rot, compounding the already pestilent conditions. With the aid of the African Creek interpreters, by April the refugees were relocated to camps along the Neosho River thirty miles north, outside Leroy, Kansas.[25]

Indian Office officials observed that the Indians not only shared their camps with the blacks but "treat[ed] them as their equals." In February 1862, Surgeon Campbell counted fifty-three African Creeks who were formerly slaves and thirty-eight African Creeks who had been freedmen in the Creek camps. G. C. Snow, the Seminole agent, counted sixty African Seminoles among the first refugees in Kansas. More African Creeks and Seminoles eventually made their way to Kansas as the first wave of refugees abandoned their homes in the Creek country during the winter of 1861-1862. The total number rose to near 300 by the early spring of 1862. Snow observed that the majority of African Seminoles claimed to be free, were intelligent, and spoke English. He also said they knew how to do common work on the farm, "but, it is evident that they have not been brought up to labor like those among the whites."

Snow's comment on the blacks from the Indian nations would be echoed by other white observers who came in contact with the African Indians during the Civil War years. These onlookers saw a significant difference in the way that African Creeks and other African Indians carried themselves when compared to African Americans from the Southern states. They were more independent and shared cultural traits with the Indians that made their ways seem strange to African Americans and Anglo Americans alike.[26] The attitudes and actions of the African Creeks showed the falsehood of the propaganda in the Southern press that blacks were naturally subservient.

The African Creek role as translators and middlemen between whites and Indians became even more important as the Loyal Indians and their black allies declared their desire to return to the Indian territory as Union volunteers. Almost immediately after their arrival in Kansas, the refugee chiefs Opothleyahola and Halleck Tustenuggee (a Seminole chief) sent a letter to President Lincoln promising to "sweep the rebels before us like a terrible fire on the prairie" if provided with the means to do so.[27] General Hunter, in cooperation with Commissioner of Indian Affairs William P. Dole and Southern [Indian] Superintendent William S. Coffin, began to enroll Creek and Seminole recruits in January 1862. It is unclear whether Hunter knew that African Creeks who were already veterans of battles such as Round Mountain, Chusto Talasah and Chustenahlah were enlisting.

Rivalries between political factions in Kansas and a jurisdictional battle between the Interior and War Departments delayed the organization of a Union Indian unit. In the midst of the quarreling in March of 1862, Hunter was reassigned to the Sea Islands of South Carolina. At his new post he began his much publicized, but unsuccessful, attempt to recruit the first black Federal soldiers. In April of 1862 the War Department finally granted the Indian Office authority to raise two Indian regiments. Recalling the harsh experiences that drove them to Kansas, the African Creeks and African Seminoles eagerly enlisted to fight the Confederates. A Kansas newspaper reported the blacks "would stick to the [Loyal] Indians through thick and thin and wished to go back to fight." An African Creek is quoted as saying that he wanted "to return to shoot his master, who is secesh" [i.e., secessionist or Confederate]."[28] When the First Indian Home Guard regiment was officially mustered into the Federal army in May of 1862, there were between twenty-five and thirty African Creeks in the regiment. These were the first black soldiers officially mustered into the Union Army during the Civil War.[29]

When the recruits were enrolled and mustered, white officers determined among other things each recruit's "complexion." The descriptions of skin coloration ran the gamut in the First Indian Regiment and show the folly of trying to made sharp racial distinctions. The term "red" and "Indian" were usually used to describe the Creek Indians, yet several African Creek recruits who later rose to prominence in the black versus Indian community were described using the same words. "Dark" was an amorphous description applied to nearly all Indians of solely Creek parentage and those African Creeks with familial and genetic ties to the Indians. Conversely, many of the recruits described as ethnically "Black" or "Negro" had purely Indian names. As Benjamin Parsons had said while counting the free African Upper Creeks before the Creek removal from Georgia to Indian Territory, "they identified with the Indians in every way except skin color." Most of the African Creek recruits were listed as "Black" "Yellow" or "African." When Lt. Charles Bowman, the mustering officer from Ft. Leavenworth, mustered the new soldiers in on May 22, 1862, they were taking persons of African descent into the army months ahead of President Lincoln's approval of such recruitment.[30]

There were ten companies in the First Indian Home Guard Regiment, the minimum number needed for such an organization. Creek Indians served as officers in eight companies. Two of the company leaders, Opothleyahola's nephew Tuckabatchee Harjo and Tulsey-Fixico, had been prominent in the Upper Creek faction before the war. Two war leaders from the Second and Third Seminole Wars captained the two Seminole companies in the organization. However, whites were appointed to the top positions in the regiment, and they would oversee its operations. Robert W. Furnas, a free-soiler from Nebraska, was appointed colonel.[31]

Though their numbers were few, the blacks in the First Indian were an essential element in the tri-racial unit. African Creeks served as interpreters as well as soldiers and provided a cultural bridge between the traditional and fully Muskogee Upper Creek soldiers—who spoke little or no English—and the white officers in the unit. They also served as clerks, orderlies, modern medicine men, soldiers, and scouts. Occupying the middle ground between white commissioned and Indian enlisted men had both advantages and hazards for the blacks as they struggled to define their role.

The first fight of First Indian Regiment (and thus the first combat experienced by regularly mustered blacks in the Federal army) came during the ill-fated Indian Expedition in the summer of 1862. The ostensible purpose of the expedition was to clear the area north of the Arkansas River in the Indian Territory of rebel troops so that the Loyal Indian and black refugees in Kansas could return to their homes. Six thousand white troops were detailed to the expedition to aid the two thousand Indian and black soldiers from the First and Second Indian Home Guard regiments.[32]

After months of preparation the Indian expedition finally headed south on June 25, 1862. Superintendent Coffin described how the soldiers in the First Indian prepared themselves for battle: "The Indians foolishly physic themselves nearly to death, dance all night, and then jump into the river just at daylight to make themselves bulletproof. They have followed this now for over two weeks, and have no doubt caused many deaths."[33] The rancid bacon for the Indian Office provided the starving refugees was probably responsible for more deaths than the ritual cleansing in the chilly water.

Whatever Coffin thought of their preparations for battle, the soldiers in the First Indian were ready to return to their country and "sweep the rebels before them." The white troops on the expedition were less enthusiastic. White and Indian troops set up separate camps and marched in separate details. Lt. Luman Tenney of the Second Ohio Calvary visited the Indian camp, where he saw a ritual ball game that he found quite interesting. But other white soldiers expressed their disgust at the "primeval customs" seen in the Indian camp. They were also surprised to see black soldiers with the Indians and remarked at how they "mixed freely" with one another. While most white soldiers tried to keep their social distance from the blacks and Indians, the officers had to maintain close contact with the African Creeks in order to communicate with the men of their command. Colonel William Weer, the commander of the expedition, issued orders that "whenever a detail of Indians is made from the Brigade for any duty whatever, the necessary number of Interpreters and guides will be named to accompany each detail." Interpreters invariably meant African Creeks, as they were essentially the only soldiers in camp who spoke both Creek and English.[34]

The Indian and African allies routed the Confederates at all three important engagements during the expedition. At Locust Grove on July 3, 1862, Wattles and Ellithorpe led the First Indian Home Guard Regiment in a surprise attack at dawn on a rebel encampment. The action captured Stand Watie's entire supply train, killed 50 rebel soldiers and captured 116, including the Confederate train commander, Col. J. J. Clarkson, and the supply officer. The white troops detailed to support the Indians refused to join the attack. They felt that the element of surprise had been lost after Colonel Weer, allegedly in a drunken stupor, had careened out onto the open prairie below the enemy camp in his ambulance while the troops were forming the attack. It was said that the only shot fired in anger by the white Federal troops at the battle was one that wounded the First Indian's surgeon, Andrew Holladay.[35]

However, the next day the white troops claimed responsibility for the victory, and most of the troops spent the national holiday celebrating with whiskey. In their drunken revelry, the white troops, who had sat on their hands at Locust Grove, decided to "throw a few shells over the Indian camp as a test to see how they would stand the fire of the big guns." They laughed when the Indians fled into the bush for protection. The incident only aggravated existing tensions between the white and Indian troops, which steadily worsened as supplies ran low, the heat rose, and the supply of good water dried up. In the following week, the African and Indian allies scouted the area. Ellithorpe led 250 First Indian soldiers on another dawn attack, this time at Sand Town Ford. No white troops were even present this time. The enemy was again stampeded. Meanwhile, the thousands of white troops contributed to the demise of the expedition by staying in camp, consuming the dwindling rations, and swilling whiskey before taking part in a mutiny by Colonel Saloman's supporters against Colonel Weer. The ineffectual soldiers returned to Kansas on July 18.[36]

The Indian troops were left behind to cover the retreat of the white troops and hold the region, if possible. Both Ellithorpe and Phillips reported that the men were eager to stay and defend the area in spite of their meager rations and the unrelenting 100 degree heat. Encouraged by this, Major Phillips led the newly created and newly arrived Third Indian Home Guard and a contingent of the First Indian against the rebels at Bayou Menard on July 25. The Indian troops defeated the rebels once again in a swift and well executed surprise attack. The Indian and African allies had succeeded in pushing the demoralized rebels south of the Arkansas River and holding the area. But, supplies exhausted and little hope of getting any in the near future, Colonel Furnas and other white officers wavered in their commitment to hold the Indian country "at all costs." Finally, after getting orders from Colonel Saloman to fall back, and feeling that the Indian troops were finally also approaching mutiny, Furnas ordered a retreat to Kansas.[37]

When Gen. James G. Blunt, the District of Kansas commander, learned that Colonel Saloman had deposed his superior officer and ordered the expedition to retreat, he immediately ordered the Indian units to stop and hold their ground. Either the order came too late or was ignored. In any case, the Indian regiments began to drift back to the refugee camps at Leroy. Meanwhile, Colonel Furnas had become disgusted with the expedition, left the regiment without specific orders, and returned to his home in Nebraska. He tendered his resignation to Secretary of War Edwin Stanton and stated his reasons: "I have always doubted the propriety and the policy of arming and placing in the field Indians . . . All communication has been through interpreters, all of whom are ignorant and uneducated Negroes, who have been raised among the Indians and possess to a

General
James A. Blunt

Generals in Blue

great degree their peculiar characteristics. The commander has but little assurance that orders are correctly given . . . or understood."[38]

Furnas, who had stayed away from the fighting, saw using the African Creek middlemen as a problem because they often identified with the needs of the Indians. However, Ritchie, Ellithorpe, and Phillips, the white officers who had been in combat, saw how well the Indian-African alliance worked in action against the enemy and judged it successful.[39]

The wartime contributions of the African Creek have seldom been recognized or rewarded. Yet African Creeks and other black soldiers in the three U.S. Indian Regiments and the First and Second Kansas Colored played a vital part in the Civil War in the Indian Territory, Arkansas, and Missouri. The men of the Second Kansas Colored, in particular, made a critical difference in the 1863 Battle of Honey Springs, the turning point of the war in Indian Territory. Many of the future leaders of the post-war Creek freedmen community came from these regiments. The rigors of war tested the bond, but the African Creek–Loyal Creek alliance survived to play an important part in the Creek Nations' politics in the post-war era. African Creeks sacrificed much for their service in the Indian and the black regiments, but they eventually won their freedom. The testament to that sacrifice and how it was linked to that of the Native Americans in the Creek Nation can be seen at the Fort Gibson National Cemetery, where the graves of the African Creeks and Creek Indian soldiers lie side by side.

NOTES

The author wishes to acknowledge the advice of his advisor at the University of Arkansas-Fayetteville, Dr. Elliott West, and the assistance of David L. Littlefield at the Native American Press archives at the University of Arkansas-Little Rock.

1. Kenneth W. Porter, *The Negro on the American Frontier* (New York: Arno Press and the *New York Times*, 1971), 467-468.

2. Daniel F. Littlefield, Jr., *Africans and Creeks: From the Colonial Period to the Civil War* (Westport, CT: Greenwood Press, 1979), 234-6.

3. United States Census Bureau, Population Schedules of the Eighth Census of the U.S. 1860: Arkansas and Indian Lands, "Non-Citizens, Creek Nation," National Archives Microfilm Publication, Microcopy M653, Reel 52 (Washington, 1967) passim; hereafter cited as M653; Ira Berlin, *Slaves Without Masters: The Free Negro in the Antebellum South* (New York: The New Press, 1974), 136-139; Creek Laws, 124-133, Grant Foreman Collection, Indian Archives Division, Oklahoma Historical Society, Oklahoma City, hereafter cited as Creek Laws followed by law number; *Van Buren Press*, March 8, 1861, 2:1; March 27, 1861, 2:2; April 3, 1861, 2:1-3; Littlefield, 235-236.

4. Althea Bass, *The Story of Tullahassee* (Oklahoma City: Semco Color Press, 1960), 90; William Robertson to Nancy Thompson, March 1, 1861, Series II, Box 19, Folder 5, Alice Robertson Collection, Special Collections, McFarlin Library, University of Tulsa, Tulsa, Oklahoma; Debo, 142-6.

5. Carter Blue Clark, "Opothleyohola and the Creeks During the Civil War," in *Indian Leaders: Oklahoma's First Statesmen*, eds. H. Glenn Jordan and Thomas M. Holm, (Oklahoma City: Oklahoma Historical Society, 1979), 49-64; Angie Debo, *The Road to Disappearance: A History of the Creek Indians* (Norman: University of Oklahoma Press, 1941), 143-6.

6. Annie Heloise Abel, *The American Indian as Slaveholder and Secessionist* (1915, reprint; Lincoln: University of Nebraska, 1992), 245-246 n. 491.

7. T. Lindsay Baker and Julie P. Baker, *The WPA Oklahoma Slave Narratives* (Norman: University of Oklahoma Press, 1996), 31, 173; Littlefield, *Africans and Creeks*, 236.

8. United States War Dept., *War of the Rebellion: Compilation of the Records of the Union and Confederate Armies*, 70 vols. in 128 books and index (Washington, D.C., 1890-1901), series I, vol. 8, 5, hereafter cited as *OR*; Edwin C. McReynolds, *The Seminoles* (Norman: University of Oklahoma Press, 1957), 292-294; Baker and Baker, 112; Charles Renty, #154; Lilas Marshall , #17, Kizzie Sells, #43; Hardy Steadham, #50; Joe Sambo, #215; Billy Hawkins, #228; Scipio Barnett, #966; Records Relating to the Loyal Creek Claims, Record Group 75, Records of the Bureau of Indian Affairs, National Archives, Washington, D.C., hereafter cited with name and claim number followed by Loyal Creek Claims. I would like to thank Dr. Daniel F. Littlefield, Jr., for directing me to this valuable resource as well as giving his time, sharing his research

notes and his insights in innumerable conversations. Thanks are also due to Mr. Napoleon Davis of the Creek Freedmen's Association in Muskogee OK, who also provided me with information on the Loyal Creek Freedmen and welcomed me as a guest at the Creek Freedmen's Memorial Shrine.

9. National Archives, Enrollment Cards for the Five Civilized Tribes: Creek Freedmen, Enrollment Card #357, "Simon Brown," (National Archives Microfilm Publication M1186 Reel 85, Washington D.C., 1956); Bass, 131; William S. Robertson to Parents, Oct. 22, 1849, Box 2, File 7 and William Robertson to Unidentified, ca. Sept,. 1850, Box 3, File 8, Alice Robertson Collection, Archives and Manuscripts Division, Oklahoma Historical Society, Oklahoma City. Many thanks to William D. Welge, Director of the Archives at OHS for providing material from the Robertson Collection.

10. James L. DeGroot, "Old Timer Article," n.d., Series I, Box 1, File 3, Alice Robertson Collection, McFarlin Library, Special Collections, University of Tulsa.

11. Simon Brown #58, Loyal Creek Claims.

12. Grant Foreman, *The Five Civilized Tribes: Cherokee, Chickasaw, Choctaw, Creek, Seminole* (Norman: University of Oklahoma Press, 1934), 195; Carolyn Foreman, "North Fork Town," 81; Billy Hawkins #228, Loyal Creek Claims.

13. Gilbert Lewis #86, Loyal Creek Claims.

14. Porter, *Negro on the American Frontier*, 467-468.

15. Quintard Taylor, *In Search of the Racial Frontier: African Americans in the American West, 1528-1990* (New York: W. W. Norton, 1998), 95-96; Dudley Cornish, *The Sable Arm, Black Troops in the Union Army, 1861-1865* (Lawrence, KS: University Press of Kansas, 1987), 74-75.

16. D. N. McIntosh to John Drew, September 11, 1861, Folder 278, John Drew Collection, Archives and Manuscripts Division, Thomas R. Gilcrease Institute of American Art and History, Tulsa, Oklahoma, hereafter cited as Drew Collection.

17. "Terms of Albert Pike to Hopothleyohola, October 7, 1861," Box 15, Folder 1, Roscoe Cate Papers, Western History Collection, University of Oklahoma, Oklahoma City, Oklahoma; Stand Watie to Drew, October 21, 1861, Folder 290, Lt. Col. Samuel Checote by Sgt Maj. J. M. Perryman to Drew, October 21, 1861, Folder 289, D. H. Cooper to Motey Kanard, October 21, 1861, Folder 291, Drew Collection.

18. Moty Kanard and Echo Harjo to John Ross, October 18, 1861, in Gary E. Moulton, ed. *The Papers of John Ross, Vol.2, 1840-1866* (Norman: University of Oklahoma Press, 1985), 497; D. N. McIntosh to Cooper, October 27, 1861, Folder 296, Drew Collection.

19. *Ft. Smith Tri-Weekly Herald*, October 9, 1861, 2:1; *Van Buren Press*, November 7, 1861, 2:2; D. N. McIntosh to Douglas Cooper, October 27, 1861, Folder 296, Drew Collection.; Moty Kanard, Echo Harjo and Others to Col. D. H. Cooper, October 31, 1861, Sam Checote's Book of Records, Indian Archives Division, Oklahoma Historical Society, Oklahoma City, Oklahoma (Oklahoma Historical Society Microfilm Publication, 1980), CRN-9, hereafter cited as CRN followed by roll and frame number. Opothleyahola was nicknamed "Old Gouge" for his sharp trading practices.

20. Cooper to Moty Kanard, Echo Harjo, and Creek Chiefs, October 31, 1861, CRN 9.

21. *Van Buren Press*, November 7, 1861, 2:2; November 14, 1861, 3:2; December 5, 1861, 2: 2.

22. J. P. Evans to his wife, December 5, 1861, Folder 309, Drew Collection, Littlefield, 236; McReynolds, *Seminoles*, 301-302.

23. Gen. David A. Hunter to Adj. Gen. Lorenzo Thomas, January 15, 1862, Letters Received by the Office of Indian Affairs: 1824-1880, RG 75 (National Archives Microfilm Publications) Microcopy M234, roll 834, frame 1494, hereafter cited as M234 followed by roll number and frame number.

24. "George Cutler Report," 283, "W. G. Coffin Report," 289, 291; "A. B. Campbell Report," 295, 298; "George W. Collamore Report,"299-300, 37th Congress, 3rd session, House Executive Document 1, Report of the Secretary of the Interior: Commissioner of Indian Affairs Report 1862, hereafter cited as COIA (Commissioner of Indian Affairs) followed by year number; "A. V. Coffin Report," 307-309, COIA, 1863; "W. G. Coffin Report," 485, COIA, 1864.

25. W. G. Coffin, Southern Superintendent, Office of Indian Affairs, to W. P. Dole, Commissioner of Indian Affairs, January 15, 1862, O. S. Coffin to W. G. Coffin, January 26, 1862, J. W. Turner to Dole, February 11, 1862, Special File 201, "Loyalty of Indians in the Southern Superintendency; Mustering of Indians into Military Service for the U.S. Office of Indian Affairs, RG 75, (National Archives Microfilm Publication, Washington, D.C.), M574, Roll 59.

26. COIA, 1862, 286-87, 295-296; William Kile to William Dole, Feb. 21, 1862, M234, roll 834, frame 1548. The estimate in the number of African Creeks and African Seminoles is based on a count of the Loyal Creek Claims that listed 1861 as the date they left the Creek country combined with the numbers listed in, RG 75 Office of Indian Affairs, Claims of the Loyal Seminoles, Special File 87, National Archives Microfilm Publication M574, Roll 11, hereafter cited as M574 with file title and roll number; Wiley Britton, *The Civil War On the Border*, vol. 2 (1899 reprint, Ottawa, KS: Kansas Heritage Press, 1994), 24-25; Baker and Baker, 84.

27. *OR* 8, 534.

28. Adjutant General Lorenzo Thomas to Col. Robert W. Furnas, April 2, 1862, Records of the United States Army Adjutant General's Office, First Indian Home Guard Regimental Order Book, 1, hereafter cited as Order Book followed by page number; Gen. David A. Hunter to A. G. Lorenzo Thomas, January 15, 1862 M234, roll 834, frame 1494; *Emporia News* (Emporia, Kansas), 8 February 1862, 2.

29. National Archives, Records Group 94, Records of the Adjutant General's Office, United States War Department, First Indian Home Guard Muster Rolls, Companies A, C, E, G, H and I, May 1862, August 1862, hereafter cited as Muster Rolls, followed by company designation and date; National Archives, Records Group 94, Records of the Adjutant General's Office, War Dept., First Indian Home Guard Descriptive Book, passim, hereafter cited as Descriptive Book followed by page number.

30. Muster Rolls, Companies A, C, E, G, H, and I, May 1862, August 1862, Descriptive Book, passim; Order Book, 1-2.

31. Robert C. Farb, "The Military Career of Robert W. Furnas," *Nebraska History*, Vol. 32, no. 1 (March 1951): 19-20. I would like to thank Alan Chilton and Arnold Schofield (the bats in the belfry) at the Fort Scott National Historic Site in Fort Scott, Kansas, for alerting me to many sources having to do with the First Indian Home Guard and generously supplying me with materials from their own files. Robert Knect of the Kansas State Historical Society provided me with valuable information on the Ellithorpe Collection as well as other materials at the KSHS Archives.

32. *OR* 13, 452.

33. Coffin to Dole, April 7, 1862, M234, Roll 834, frames 1158-1159.

34. Luman Harris Tenney, *War Diary of Luman Harris Tenney: 1861-1865*, (Cleveland: Evangelical Publishing House, 1914), 16, 19; Britton, *Civil War on the Border*, 17; General Order # 6, July 13, 1862, General Order # 7, July 14, 1862, Headquarters, Indian Expedition, General Orders, Department of Missouri Book 971; Lt. W. R. Shattue to Col. Frederick Saloman, "Plat of Camp on Horse Creek" Various Lists Relating to Safeguards, Details and Other Lists, 1862-3, Department of Missouri Book 973, RG 393, Records of the U.S. Army Continental Commands National Archives Building, Washington, D.C.; Furnas to Stanton, Sept. 7, 1862, Robert W. Furnas Papers, Archives and Manuscripts Division, (Nebraska Historical Society Microfilm Publication, Lincoln, 1951), Roll 11, frames 11324-27, hereafter cited as Furnas Papers.

35. Farb, "The Military Career of Robert W. Furnas," 24-26; Albert C. Ellithorpe, Diary of A. C. Ellithorpe, July 3, 1862, hereafter cited as Ellithorpe Diary, in the private collection of Dr. Tom Sweeney, on display at General Sweeny's: A Museum of Civil War History, Republic, Missouri. I would like to thank Dr. Sweeney for his generosity in allowing me to study Ellithorpe's diary as well as to consult other materials in his private collection; COIA, 1862, 306-8.

36. Ellithorpe Diary, July 4, July 12, July 14, 1862; *Ft. Smith Bulletin*, October 30, 1862, 2: 3; Tenney Diary, 20; Issac Grause, *Four Years with Five Armies, The Army of the Frontier, the Army of the Potomac, the Army of the Ohio and the Army of the Shenandoah* (New York: Neale Pub., 1908), 84-85.

37. *OR* 13, 181-183, 511-512; Furnas to Phillips, July 30, 1862, Furnas Papers.

38. Maj. John Ritchie to Blunt, August 13, 1862, Ritchie to Lt. Col. Stephen Wattles, August 10, 1862, Department of Missouri Book 146/265-266, 1-5, 8-9, RG 393, Records of the U.S. Army Continental Commands, National Archives Building, Washington, D.C., hereafter cited as MO 146/265-266; Furnas to Stanton, Sept. 7, 1862, Furnas Papers.

39. A. C. Ellithorpe, July 12 and 14, 1862, Diary of A.C. Ellithorpe,.; *OR* 13, 181-183; Ritchie to Blunt, August 13, 1862, MO 146/265-266, 1-5.

RESERVATION AND EASTERN INDIANS
During the American Civil War, 1861-1865

Michael A. Hughes

("Nations Asunder, Part I," which appreared in the previous issue, dealt with Western Indians outside of Indian Territory during the Civil War.)

As noted in the first part of "Nations Asunder," one of the reasons for the obscurity of the Indian wars of the 1860s is that many of them took place within the overshadowing context of the American Civil War. Although relatively little has been written about native cultures during this devastating period, the Indian population living west of the ninety-fifth meridian—the line of longitude running north-south down the center of North America—has received the majority of this limited attention.

The other Indian population consisted of nations in states east of the Mississippi River and of eastern tribes relocated to reservations in and north of present-day Oklahoma. This population was largely sedentary and generally lived in, or was largely surrounded by, white communities. Whether reservation Indians, tenacious remnants of dispossessed nations, or "assimilated" members of white society, this second population usually survived more by accommodation than resistance. As a result, some 20,000 Indian Territory and eastern Indians were drawn into the Civil War as soldiers or auxiliaries of the United States or the Confederacy.

This article is their story.

I. Western Reservation Peoples and the Civil War

Until 1854, all of the "unorganized territory" of the Louisiana Purchase was designated as "Indian country" or "Indian territory." Legislation in the 1820s and 1830s defined specific tribal reservations in what are now the states of Nebraska, Kansas, and Oklahoma. Nebraska was reserved for tribes that were were already resident. Most of Kansas was used for the resettlement of tribes that lived in what became the first tier of U.S. territories west of the Mississippi. Small areas of Kansas were also partitioned off for tribes relocated from northern states east of the Mississippi River. Much of Oklahoma was reserved for the "Five Tribes" or "Five Civilized Tribes" from Southern states east of the Mississippi. However, a large "Leased District" in southwestern Oklahoma was secured from the Chickasaw and Choctaws for the settlement of "other tribes," beginning with the Wichitas. Mentions of the Indian Territory proper (versus Western "Indian territory" in general) always refer to the reserved areas in present-day Oklahoma.

There were perhaps four major factors involved in the decision of Nebraska Territory, Kansas Territory, and [Oklahoma] Indian Territory Indians to participate in the Civil War: a) the hope of preserving their reservations against pressure from citizens of neighboring states; b) internal political struggles within some nations; c) the withdrawal of U.S. Army garrisons from forts in and near Indian Territory and the accompanying suspension of federal annuity payments; and d) the complex and unstable situation created by the rival diplomatic efforts of various United States, Confederate, and Indian leaders. To this list might be added several lesser motivations such as the need for employment, the prospects of revenge upon the states responsible for Indian removal, and half-forgotten but still cherished warrior traditions.

Prior to the Civil War, the Indians of the future states of Nebraska, Kansas, and Oklahoma faced the constant threat of losing all or part of their reservations. When Kansas attained statehood in 1861, its representatives began to incessantly demand the removal of the state's Indians. Texans wanted the Comanches and Kiowas in their state removed to the Indian Territory and were

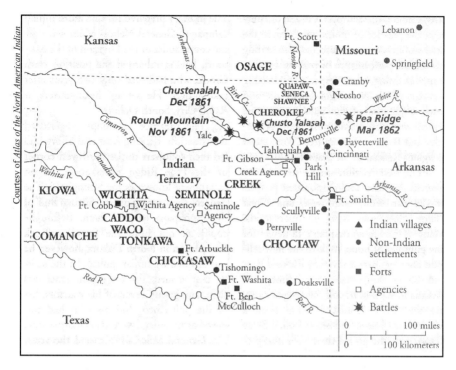

covetous of a still unassigned area north of the Red River. Similarly, citizens of Missouri and Arkansas looked forward to the day when the Cherokees' little used "Neutral Lands" and "Cherokee Outlet" in Indian Territory might be seized for white settlement.

When the Civil War began, some Indians believed that their best hope for preserving their lands might be trying either to fight or to ally with the state governments that threatened them. Unfortunately, when the union split asunder members of several Indian nations could not agree on which states might best prove friends and which enemies. The situation was complicated by the fact that factions within the nations would sometimes use alliances with either the United States or the Confederacy as a means of settling grudges with opposing factions. Such was particularly true of the much divided Cherokees, Creeks, and Seminoles and would soon become true of the Caddos, Osages, and Wichitas as well.

II. Indians of the [Oklahoma] Indian Territory

Most of the nations of the Indian Territory identified culturally with the white South. As Texas state Indian commissioners noted as their region seceded, the Five Tribes at least "declare themselves southern by geographic position, by a common interest, by their social system, and by blood, for they are rapidly becoming a nation of whites." This bond was strengthened by the fact that several popular federal Indian agents, like Douglas H. Cooper for the Chickasaw, were Southerners. The elites of many Indian Territory nations were slave holders and shared the Confederacy's interest in preserving that institution. In addition, the economies of the Five Tribes were linked to those of Arkansas and Texas, and the Cherokees had developed close social and familial ties to the citizens of western Arkansas.

The Confederacy was eager to secure alliances with the Indian Territory nations for several reasons. The Indians could provide some recruits and, equally as important, a great many beef cattle. Perhaps most significantly, the Indian Territory would serve to buffer Confederate Arkansas and Texas from military expeditions out of Union Kansas and Missouri. In their overtures to the Indian nations, Confederate Indian commissioners cleverly pointed out recent historical and political developments. For example, they noted that even though the Cherokees and Upper Creeks had assisted the U.S. Army in the Creek War (1813-1814) and that many Chickasaws had done the same in the Second Seminole War (1835-1842), the United States had ungratefully exiled these allies to the Indian Territory. The commissioners also made a good case that the anti-centralization and "states' rights" political theories of the Confederacy were highly compatible with the concept of tribal political autonomy.

On the other hand, it was difficult for the Indians of the Indian Territory to forget that Southern states (notably Alabama, Georgia, and Texas) had engineered their removal westward. Citizens of Southern states had also been guilty of notorious incidents of racism and racial violence towards Indians, even by the century's low standards of ethnic tolerance. In addition, some of the most selfless missionaries in Indian Territory had been Northerners, and many of these had encouraged anti-slavery sentiment. In the Cherokee nation, a rift was developing between a slave-holding planter class and the common Cherokees; many of the latter joined the traditionalist and abolitionist Keetoowah Society. Because Keetoowahs wore crossed straight pins as an emblem, pro-Union and anti-slavery Indians from Indian Territory would often be called "pin Indians" during the Civil War.

But even pro-Northern and pro-Union Indians felt betrayed by the withdrawal of the Regular Army from the forts of Indian Territory in April 1861. The resettled Indians of Indian Territory had implicitly been promised protection from Plains tribes like the Kiowas, Comanches, and Wichitas when forced to agree to removal from east of the Mississippi. There was considerable fear and resentment when their defenders were removed from forts in New Mexico, Kansas, and Indian territories, and from the state of Texas. The Confederacy was able to present itself as the savior of the Indian Territory as a consequence. The hope of future Confederate assistance against "wild" Indians was widespread even though the Confederate Indian treaties did not promise Confederate frontier defense until after the conclusion of the war with the Union. The Confederacy did, however, arm some groups, particularly among the Cherokees.

The withdrawal of the United States frontier garrisons was accompanied by several other disturbing events. One was the resignation of most known Indian agents. Several of the most trusted of these, such as Douglas H. Cooper, left to serve the Confederacy. Another troubling development was the suspension of annuity payments due to the tribes for the sale of their ancestral lands. This halt was caused by political and economic chaos resulting from the outbreak of war and from fears that pay shipments would be seized by Arkansas or Texas Confederates. The suspension permitted the Confederacy to play upon the Indian Territory Indians' growing sense of betrayal. The fact that Confederate troops from Texas had almost immediately occupied the vacated posts enabled the Confederacy to exert a subtle pressure on the Five Tribes at the same time.

Confederate Indian commissioner Albert Pike became the key player in the near chaotic political conditions in Indian Territory in 1861. Pike was a Massachusetts-born poet and attorney who impressed the Indians with his dignity, eloquence, and proven interest in their culture and well-being. He was one of the few whites with knowledge of some southern Indian languages, and he had recently won a major financial settlement for the Creek nation. The timing of Pike's arrival in Indian Territory was nearly perfect. As he visited the Indian nations, word was received of the Confederate victory in the war's first major battle at Manassas (Bull Run) on July 21, 1861. Midway through his journey, the Indians also learned of the Federal defeat in the first significant action west of Mississippi at Wilson's Creek, Missouri on August 10, 1861.

Bolstered by what appeared to be the rising prospects of the Confederacy, Pike's negotiations were a complete success.

Pike negotiated a total of nine treaties with Indian Territory Indians during the summer and fall of 1861. Four were with the "Five Civilized Tribes." Two were negotiated in the Leased District, one with eleven signers for small nations living there, the other with signers for the Plains Comanches. Three were with four tribes not well represented in the Indian Territory. These treaties obligated the Confederacy to recognize existing treaties and reservation boundaries and uphold the tribes' rights to self-government. The nations on their part agreed to surrender land for military facilities and raise levies of troops for Confederate service, though such troops would be paid by the Confederacy and would not be required to serve outside of Indian Territory "without their consent." The last condition made the tribes technically protectorates as much as allies. As far as the Indian nations were concerned, the treaties were superior to almost all of those previously offered by the United States. Government officials in Richmond appear to have been sincere about honoring the treaty conditions. However, military department commanders west of the Mississippi thought nothing of ordering Indian Territory troops outside of the territory without consultation. Pike would later resign his position as a brigadier general in protest over the practice.

It is difficult to overstate the magnitude of Pike's diplomatic accomplishments. But much about the treaties is misleading. First, over half of the treaties were signed by individuals who represented only one faction within their band or nation. This was hardly novel—very few nineteenth century Indian treaties were signed by individuals who represented a consensus within their nation. Second, five treaties were with Indian nations that had reservations in present-day Kansas, not the [Oklahoma] Indian Territory. The persons who signed for the Delaware, Osage, Quapaw, Seneca, and Shawnee nations were members of small breakaway groups. The principal chiefs of these five nations probably did not know until much later that the treaties had been signed. The same is likely true of the leaders of the five divisions of Comanches termed the "Comanches of the Prairies and Staked Plains." Finally, Pike or his interpreters were confused about eight of the "nations" that signed at the Wichita Agency on August 12. The eight names actually represented bands or divisions within three tribal confederacies, those of the Caddo, Wichita, and Hasinai. Rather than twenty-one nations, perhaps as few as ten could be said to have contracted alliances with the Confederacy. On the other hand, the treaties for the "Five

Tribes" were signed by appropriate authorities, and the "Five Tribes" comprised over two-thirds of the residents of the [Oklahoma] Indian Territory.

A. The Cherokees and the "Cherokee Brigade" (Cherokee name [adapted]: Tsalagi)

The Cherokee—eastern and Indian Territory—were by far the Indian people most heavily recruited by both the Confederacy and the United States. The Indian Territory Cherokees were also perhaps the most thoroughly divided of all Indian nations during the Civil War. Much of the rivalry dated back to the rancor created by the Treaty of New Echota, which sold the Cherokees' Georgia reservation and required them to move to Indian Territory. The treaty had been signed by a decidedly minority faction of the nation, a faction known as the "Ridge," "removal," or "treaty" faction. This group was led by members of the Ridge family and Elias Boudinot. Their signatures made them subject to death under Cherokee law, and after the resettlement John Ridge, Major Ridge, and Boudinot were murdered by persons unknown. Principal Chief John Ross, who had opposed the treaty, decried the killing but was guilty by association in the minds of the survivors of the Ridge faction. Another division in the Cherokee nation complemented that of Ridge versus Ross but was less well defined. This was a gap between elite Cherokees acculturated to white Southern society, some of whom were only partially Cherokee in ancestry, and traditionalist Cherokees, many of whom were fully Cherokee by birth. A number of the latter were members of the Keetoowah Society, a group with mixed elements of traditionalism, moralism, and abolitionism.

In the Indian Territory, planter and attorney Stand Watie, the brother of Elias Boudinot, assumed leadership of the old Ridge faction after the assassinations. He also was a representative of the pro-South and mixed ancestry members of the nation. Ross was equally a member of the slave-holding elite but cultivated close ties to the traditionalists and to common Cherokees. As the secession crisis began to divide the eastern states, Watie moved quickly to raise troops for the Confederacy. He apparently did this partly out of conviction, partly out of hopes of toppling the Ross faction from power and taking control of the nation.

Ross maintained that Cherokee treaties with the United States, however evil, were sacrosanct. He also argued that if the Cherokees were to be genuinely

Brigadier General
Stand Watie

Generals in Gray

autonomous, they must remain neutral. The chief managed to steer the Cherokees clear of a Confederate alliance during Albert Pike's first diplomatic visit in July 1861. However, the other four of the "Five Tribes" soon signed treaties, and many Cherokees expressed support for the Confederacy during the summer. Ross concluded that the tribe's best hope was to achieve some type of consensus and that his own prospects for leadership depended on supporting popular demand. Ross called for a mass meeting in August to decide the issue of alliance with the Confederacy. The attendees unanimously voted for such an agreement and authorized their elected officials to proceed with negotiations. On October 7, 1861, the Cherokees became the last Indian nation to sign a treaty with the Confederacy.

Perhaps the best indicator of the rivalries and tensions within the Cherokee nation is the story of its two first regiments. In early 1861, months before the first shots of the war, Watie was urged by a white son-in-law and an Arkansas attorney to begin raising pro-Confederate "defense" companies. In July, Watie was commissioned a Confederate colonel by Brig. Gen. Benjamin McCulloch in western Arkansas. This coincided with a mass rally of Southern sympathizers among the "Six Tribes." Watie used the occasion to begin recruiting and organizing volunteers, and he had his first Cherokee Mounted Volunteers enrolled around July 12. Like Watie, many members of the unit strongly sympathized with the Southern states culturally and politically. Most of its officers and a number of the enlisted men were not fully Cherokee by birth. In addition, because of many social and economic connections between the regiments' officers and citizens of neghboring states, the organization contained white recruits from northwestern Arkansas and southwestern Missouri. Watie's regiment would remain utterly faithful to Watie and the Confederacy, with most of its men serving through several enlistments. The regiment would be with Watie at Doaksville, Indian Territory, on June 23, 1865, when he became the last Confederate general to surrender.

It doubtless galled Watie that even though his was the first Cherokee regiment to be formed, it was an organization influenced by Ross that would be designated the First Cherokee Mounted Rifles. Unlike Watie's regiment, the Mounted Rifles was originally authorized by the Cherokee government rather than the Confederacy. When the August mass meeting called for separation from the United States, the Cherokee Executive Committee began forming a regiment for "national defense." The unit was enrolled on October 4, 1861. Most of the officers were selected by Ross in a last attempt by the neutral faction of the tribe to remain in control of events. The Mounted Rifles' colonel was John Drew, a wealthy salt works owner. Though related to Ross through marriage, he was respected by the Ridge-Watie faction and like Watie was pro-Confederate and of mixed ancestry. However, many of Drew's men were of fully Cherokee parentage. Also, a good number of them were members of the Keetoowah Society and/or the Loyal League, the latter a group that considered anyone who had signed the old removal treaty or the new Confederate alliance treaty a traitor.

A few individual Cherokees were reported to have been present at the August 1861 fight at Wilson's Creek. However, enrolled Cherokee units did not appear in battle until December 9, 1861. On that date, Colonel Douglas H. Cooper, acting commander of the first "Indian brigade," ordered Watie's and Drew's regiments into the second battle against the followers of the traditionalist Creek leader Opothleyahola (see below). Both before and after the battle, many of Drew's man, disturbed at having been asked to kill their Creek "brothers," deserted. Both Cherokee regiments responded when Albert Pike requested Indian assistance in a campaign that culminated in the Battle of Pea Ridge, Arkansas, on March 6-8, 1861. However, Indian participation in the battle was minimal. The two Cherokee regiments backed the capture of a Missouri battery by Texans the first day of the battle, but were otherwise little engaged.

In July 1862, Federal troops out of Kansas launched the first attempt to recover the Indian Territory. When they entered the Cherokee nation, all of the remaining men of Drew's Confederate regiment except one company deserted and joined the enemy. The Second Cherokee Mounted Rifles is considered the only regiment in the Civil War to have been destroyed by deserting to the other side. Most of the men, including two of John Ross's sons, eventually joined the Indian Home Guard regiments. The Union Cherokees spent the duration of the war primarily fighting engagements against forces that included Watie's old regiment. The Confederate Cherokees replaced Drew's regiment in December of 1862 by consolidating the single remaining company of Drew's regiment with nine companies from other organizations.

As the conversion of Drew's regiment indicates, many Cherokees became neutral or pro-Union in sympathy. As many as 7,000 such Cherokees fled to Kansas to avoid supporting the Confederacy or to avoid retaliation by rival factions. Cherokees provided the greatest number of members—2,200—in the three Union Indian Home Guard regiments. In February of 1863, just four months after signing a treaty with the Confederacy, the Cherokee National Council repudiated the document and proclaimed its loyalty to the United States. The Cherokee nation also banished slavery, almost two years before the United States did so. The Watie faction responded by declaring Watie to be the tribal chief and forming a rival legislature. When the war ended, Watie lobbied for federal recognition of two separate Cherokee reservations in Indian Territory. However, he was outmaneuvered one last time by the aging and dying Ross, and the Cherokees officially remained one tribe.

Though the last tribe of the Indian Territory to enter the Civil War, the western Cherokees suffered more terribly than any nation of the territory. Over a quarter of Cherokee Union soldiers died of battle or disease, a higher percentage than that of any state's military population. The roughly 21,000 Cherokees in the Indian Territory in 1861were reduced to 13,866 enumerated members. In addition, as part of the only mass confiscation to follow the Civil War, the Cherokees were forced to liquidate most of their territorial possessions. The government required that the Cherokees themselves broker the sale of the Cherokee Outlet. The land was theoretically to be used to settle other Indian nations, but it was instead given to white settlers. The Cherokee Strip and "Neutral Lands" of Kansas were sold by the federal government at auction.

B. The Chickasaws and the Choctaw and Chickasaw Regiment (Chickasaw name for Chickasaw: Chicksa *or* Chickasha; *Choctaw name for Choctaw:* Chockta)

At the time of the Civil War, the Chickasaws and Choctaws were perhaps more fully acculturated with the white South than any other Indian nation. They also had strong economic ties to Arkansas and Texas and a substantial investment in slaves. Other than experiencing the departure of some Choctaw families that accompanied Opothleyahola to Kansas, the Choctaw and Chickasaw nations were the least disunited of the Five Tribes during the war. The two linguistically related nations were closely associated in Indian Territory and had signed their alliance treaty with the Confederacy jointly.

The Choctaws and Chickasaws also cooperated in forming a Confederate regiment in the summer of 1861. The colonel was a much respected Southerner, Douglas H. Cooper, who had been U.S. agent to the Choctaw nation before the war. He would be the only white commander of an Confederate Indian Territory regiment. After Cooper was promoted to brigadier general and assigned as commander of the Indian Territory, planter Tandy Walker became the regiment's colonel.

The organization's members were some of the most tenacious fighters from the territory and fought in more campaigns and battles than any other Confederate Indian regiment. Like the Cherokee regiments, the Choctaw-Chickasaw Regiment fought at least one battle in defense of the neighboring state of Arkansas. In the spring of 1864, a Federal expedition set out from Little Rock, Arkansas, in support of the Union Red River campaign in Louisiana. When the Louisiana campaign faltered, the Confederate high command west of the Mississippi focused on the Union expedition in Arkansas. Brig. Gen. Samuel Bell Maxey, who commanded the Confederate Department of the Indian Territory, was ordered to assist. As Pike had earlier, Maxey overstepped his authority and decided to lead Indian troops over the boundary of Indian Territory. Maxey's Texas brigade and the 700 men of the Chickasaw-Choctaw regiment were joined with Louisiana and Arkansas troops to form a large force that would attempt to wreak Federal supply operations in southwestern Arkansas.

On April 18, 1864, at Poison Spring, the Confederates struck a large wagon train that had been foraging corn for troops occupying Camden, Arkansas. Many in the train's escort were trapped, particularly members of the First Kansas Colored Volunteers. One hundred and seventeen black troops were killed as they tried to escape or surrender. Several observers noted that the Choctaw-Chickasaw regiment led the slaughter. One Confederate private stated, "You ought to see Indians fight Negroes, kill and scalp them. Let me tell you, I never expected to see so many dead Negroes again." The Choctaws and Chickasaws may have been seeking revenge for the heavy casualties that the First Kansas had inflicted on their Texas comrades at the Battle of Honey Springs the previous year. A later story that they were seeking revenge for heavy foraging by the First Kansas on the Choctaw Reservation in early 1864 does not seem to have much evidence to support it.

Though the Chickasaw and Choctaw reservations were far enough south to escape the worst of the wartime devastation in Indian country, thousands of members of these nations were refugees in Confederate Texas at the war's end. The government forced the two nations to sell the Leased District and over one third of the reservation they had held jointly prior to the war. For the latter acreage, the two tribes received perhaps a quarter of the market value.

C. The Creeks and Opothleyahola's Retreat (Creek name Muskogee *or* Muscogee)

Like the Cherokees, the "Creeks" (i.e., Muskogees) were seriously divided between adherents to neutrality or the Union and advocates for the Confederacy. The rift in the Creek nation was also similar to the divide among the Cherokees in that support for the United States or the Confederacy was determined as much by intertribal rivalry as it was by genuine conviction. At the time of the Civil War, the Creek nation was still healing from several old disputes between members of the former Upper Creek towns and Lower Creek towns of the Muskogee confederacy. In the Creek War of 1813-1814, the more traditional Upper Creeks had risen against white Georgians whom the United States had permitted to infiltrate Creek territory. However, a number of Lower Creeks led by Chief William McIntosh had fought alongside volunteers of the United States in defeating their fellow Creeks. The animosity became worse in 1825 when McIntosh accepted what was viewed as a bribe and signed the treaty removing the Creeks to west of the Mississippi. The chief was promptly executed by the Upper Creeks in retaliation. A major negotiator and power broker for the Upper Creeks, Opothleyahola, delayed the tribe's removal as long as possible, but even he and his supporters eventually capitulated and signed a modified removal agreement.

In the Indian Territory, the councils for the Upper and Lower Creeks finally united, and the nation functioned under a balance of power between the forces of Opothleyahola and those of Daniel N. McIntosh, the son of William McIntosh. By 1861, the McIntosh faction was even more assimilated into Southern white society than formerly. As a result, McIntosh's followers sympathized with the Confederacy. Opothleyahola, by contrast, had never forgiven the Southern states for their role in Indian removal. In addition, he adhered to traditional Muskogee culture and religion. The traditionalist Keetoowah movement had gained some strength among Opothleyahola's followers, though without much of the anti-slavery sentiment it had had among its Cherokee founders.

When offered a treaty of alliance with the Confederacy in July 1816, Chief Moty Kinniard and the McIntosh faction gladly signed. They also began to create a Creek Confederate military unit. The First Creek Regiment was organized by McIntosh on August 19, 1861. Many of the officers were friends or relatives of the McIntosh family, and many were descendants of Lower versus Upper Creeks. The regiment also contained some Seminoles. Chilly McIntosh, Daniel's half brother, left the regiment in the early fall of 1861 to form and lead a new unit, the Creek Battalion. In 1862, the battalion would be expanded to form the Second Creek Regiment.

Other Creeks maintained that the treaty and the formation of the First Creek Regiment were unlawful and elected a rival chief. Opothleyahola meanwhile declared his personal neutrality. Neutral and pro-Union Indians soon began to take shelter on Opothleyahola's 2,000-acre farm. By fall, there were approximately 9,000 refugees there. These included many Creeks, about half of the Seminole nation, and some Osage and Quapaw families. Though sometimes termed an "army," perhaps only 1,500 of the men on the farm were prepared to defend themselves.

A number of "African Creeks" and "African Seminoles," both free and still in bondage, were also encamped on Opothleyahola's farm. Creek slaves had possessed an unusually high degree of freedom of mobility, and there was a much higher percentage of freedmen among the Creeks than among white Southerners. When the McIntosh-Southern faction of the tribe allied with the Confederacy, they agreed to enact stringent codes for the control of slaves and to force all free blacks into servitude. Although Opothleyahola was himself a slave holder and did not encourage any slaves to flee their masters, he did not intend for any of the African Creeks or Seminoles to fall into the hands of the Confederate faction. In addition, Opothleyahola may have been influenced by the fact that many of the blacks had some Creek parentage. As a result of

Opothleyahola's feelings, as many of 700 of the African Creeks and African Seminoles were armed in some fashion.

Douglas H. Cooper was at this time in command of the troops within the Indian Territory. Cooper sent several messages to Opothleyahola requesting that he swear allegiance to the Confederacy, but he received no reply. The McIntosh faction became more and more concerned about the prospect of armed resistance from Opothleyahola's people. In November, Cooper set out with around 1,400 men—most of his own Choctaw-Chickasaw regiment, all organized Creek and Seminole Confederate forces, and some Texas cavalry. Cooper intended to force Opothleyahola to submit or else he would "drive him and his party from the country." Cooper motivated the Creek Confederates by promising to seize and sell all blacks found with Opothleyahola to benefit the McIntosh government's treasury. McIntosh reportedly represented the campaign as a holy crusade against the "pagan" Opothleyahola.

By the time Cooper set out, Opothleyahola's people were already afoot on a mass exodus northward. They hoped to take refuge among Cherokees sharing their sentiments. Cooper's men twice leapt upon deserted encampments before blundering into an occupied one near Round Mountain on November 19, 1861. Opothleyahola's men forced Cooper's cavalry advance back onto his main force, and darkness prevented Cooper from effectively counterattacking. When the Confederates moved forward in strength the next morning, they found yet another abandoned camp.

By December 9, Opothleyahola's forces were located at a defensible position within a curve of Bird Creek, north of Tulsey Town (present-day Tulsa). By this time, his groups' goal had become to escape with their lives to Union-held Kansas. The battle that would take place that day would be known to Cherokees as Chusto-Talasah or Caving Banks, and to whites as Horseshoe Bend (not to be confused with Andrew Jackson's victory over the Creeks at Horseshoe Bend in 1814). Cooper had by this time been joined by the two Confederate Cherokee regiments. After four hours of fighting on the creek, a Texas cavalry squadron outflanked Opothleyahola's position, and an attack by the Choctaw-Chickasaw Regiment gained a foothold within the bend. However, when the refugees finally fled, the Confederates did not have sufficient ammunition to follow up their victory. In addition, a number of members of Drew's Cherokee regiment had deserted to their fellow Keetoowahs and traditionalists among the fleeing Creeks.

Cooper resupplied, reorganized, and reinforced his command, and then he set out again with 1,400 men. On Christmas day, Confederate scouts located Opothleyahola's encampments on a small bend of Hominy Creek. The people there were starving and were suffering terribly from an icy turn in the weather. Cooper's forces attacked at noon on December 26. Opothleyahola's men retreated as slowly as possible up the side of a brushy hill, trying to create time for the women and children to escape before being routed. The engagement would later give the current geographical names "Battle Creek" and "Patriot Hills" to its location. By the time the defeated mass reached Kansas, battle, exposure, and starvation had taken the lives of at least 2,000 people. Opothleyahola himself would soon die as an exile within Union lines. Federal forces in Kansas were not prepared for the onslaught of refugees and considered them a liability. Eventually, the dire condition of the survivors would be a factor in the formation of three Union Indian Home Guard Regiments in the spring and summer of 1862.

Opothleyahola's retreat marked several significant "firsts" in American history. Cooper's campaign was the first time that war was conducted against a primarily civilian population within the United States. The retreat was one of the first mass migrations or dislocations of people in the United States as the result of a military conflict. The three engagements were the first Civil War battles fought in what many people have considered the "true" or "far" West, i.e., the region west of the ninety-fifth meridian. Finally, because of the presence of the Creek and Seminole freedmen, the retreat was the first occasion during the Civil War in which Americans of African descent fought for their own freedom.

Like the Cherokee nation, the Creek nation ended the war divided and impoverished. Its people were forced by the United States to sell approximately 60 percent of their former reservation. The tribe long remained perhaps the most divided in Indian Territory. Some Creeks also maintained the longest opposition to assimilation into white society in the Indian Territory. The last armed resistance of Creek traditionalists would not end until 1909.

D. The Seminoles (from Muskogee Seminola; Creek name: Kaniúksalsi)

The majority of Seminoles may have been genuinely neutral at the beginning of the Civil War. However, a pro-Confederate faction, led by elected chief and Seminole minister John Jumper, signed a Confederate treaty of alliance on August 1, 1861. Jumper also formed and led the Confederate Seminole Battalion. As the fairly small Seminole nation was split over the treaty, it was never possible to enroll enough men to field a Seminole regiment.

Over the next few months following the signing, around half of the nation deserted their homes and went to the camp of the Creek chief Opothleyahola. After Opothleyahola's refugees fled to Kansas, they were joined there by several prominent pro-Union Seminoles. These included John Chupco, a town chief who had refused to sign the treaty, and Billy Bowlegs, who ironically had been one of the fiercest opponents of the United States in the Second Seminole War. Both men enlisted their followers in the Indian Home Guard regiments. Chupco also served as a rival chief to John Jumper during the war, and he would be legitimately elected chief when peace was restored.

Despite the services of Chupco and the Seminole Union veterans, the Seminole nation were severely treated by the United States following the war. The Seminoles were relocated to an area around 10 percent of the size of the one they had formerly occupied. They were also forced to purchase the new homeland from the Creeks for three times what they were paid for the land they relinquished.

E. The Leased District Indians

The so-called "other tribes" occupying the Leased District were generally groups that had either been pushed out of Texas or dislocated within Oklahoma. There were also a few Delawares, Osages, Quapaws, Senecas, and Shawnees from Kansas reservations living in the district. Representatives of all these different groups signed one of Albert Pike's treaties of alliance with the Confederacy in August of 1861. However, some of the Indians in the district had developed a dislike and distrust of the neighboring state of Texas, which to them represented the Confederacy. Most of the Delaware, Quapaw, Osage, Seneca, and Shawnee Indians of the district were actually neutral or pro-Union. Many fled and fought with the Creek chief Opothleyahola on his retreat to Kansas in late 1861. Only the Tonkawas and some of the Caddos remained loyal to the Confederacy. The loyalties and wartime location of most of the Comanches and Wichitas of the Leased District are uncertain, though many Comanches at least may have moved to Texas during the war.

1. *The Tonkawas* (Tonkawa name: *Titska watitch*) originally lived in central Texas but were moved to the Leased District of Indian Territory—now west central Oklahoma—in 1859. During the Civil War, they served as Confederate scouts against Federal Indians in the Indian Territory. In October 1862, a force of pro-Union refugee Indians armed in Kansas destroyed the Confederate offices at Wichita Agency in the Leased District. Reportedly, that night these Indians were horrified on hearing a report that the Tonkawa village to the south was about to revert to the practice of ritual cannibalism with a captive. The pro-Union Indians were also aware of the village's political loyalties. The next morning the force attacked and massacred 135-150 of the 300 Tonkawas present. The surviving Tonkawas fled to Confederate-held Fort Arbuckle and in 1863 retreated to a refuge in Texas. There the Tonkawas occasionally served as scouts for the Confederates and the Texas militia against the Comanches, who were traditional enemies of the Tonkawas. After the war, the Tonkawas were again utilized as scouts against the Comaches and Kiowas, this time as employees of the U.S. Army. It may have been this service which enabled the Tonkawas to remain in Texas until 1884, when they were finally returned to Indian Territory.

2. *The Caddos* (adaptation of the Caddo band name *Kadohadacho*) were also recent residents of the Leased District of [Oklahoma] Indian Territory, many having fled there from a Texas reservation following a massacre committed by white settlers in 1859. Despite this, a faction of the tribe signed the Confederate alliance treaty. The Caddos had traditionally been only a loose confederation, and their still-evolving sense of nationhood was partially based on their mutual opposition to external enemies. The signing of the alliance treaty apparently caused division among the Caddo people. One of the chiefs, Show-e-at (known to whites as "Little Boy" or "George Washington") formed a scout and ranger company on behalf of the Confederacy. The company at one point did battle with a group of what were termed "renegade" Caddos, but Show-e-at's unit primarily served to protect the Indian Territory from raids by nomadic tribes from the West. In one engagement Show-e-at's men fought a group of Kiowas and Mescalero Apaches, and in another incident they battled a group of Comanches.

III. Kansas and Nebraska Reservation Indians Recruited as United States Troops, Auxiliaries, and Scouts

[Thomas W. Dunlay's *Wolves for the Blue Soldiers: Indian Scouts and Auxiliaries with the United States Army, 1869-1890* is a particularly useful source of information on western Indians recruited as scouts.]

A. *The Delawares* (*Delaware name*: Lenni Lenape)—The Delawares were originally eastern Indians. The Unami divisions and a few of the Munsee divisions were forced westwards by stages until by 1830 they were on a reservation in northeastern Kansas. There was also a small band of Delawares who had been living in the Leased District of the [Oklahoma] Indian Territory since 1859. The latter were descendants of an old breakaway group known as the "Absentee Delawares." A few members of the Absentees in the Leased District signed a Confederate alliance treaty with Albert Pike in August of 1861. However, the alliance appears to have been unpopular and was opposed by the Absentees' chief, the famous scout Black Beaver. Confederate Indians responded by destroying his farm and offering a bounty for his head. A number of the Leased District Delawares then fled to Union lines in Kansas. Some would fight alongside with the Creek chief Opothleyahola on his retreat to Kansas in late 1861.

Meanwhile, the reservation Delawares in Kansas declared their loyalty to the Union as early as October of 1861. Western Delawares had been hired as scouts for military mapping and peacekeeping expeditions since the 1840s. On October 4, 1861, a group of fifty-four of them became the first Indians to be mustered into United States service in the Civil War. By 1862, 170 of 201 eligible western Delawares had enrolled. Though left nearly destitute by the pre-Civil War fighting in Kansas, the Delawares also provided assistance for Cherokee and Creek Union refugees.

B. *The Osages*—Originally a prairie and woodlands people in what is now Missouri, the Osages had held a narrow reservation in southern Kansas since 1808. The Osage tribe was already in a state of crisis when Civil War began. Pro-slavery and anti-slavery guerrillas had looted the Osage Reservation during the "Bleeding Kansas" fighting of the 1850s. In addition, the national ascendancy of the Republican party in 1860 increased the political power of Kansas settlers. The state's representatives were intent on dismembering as much as possible of the Osage and other Indian reservations in Kansas. When Confederate Indian commissioner Albert Pike visited the Cherokee reservation in October 1861, visiting representatives of the Osage nation, like several of their neighbors, signed a treaty of alliance with the Confederacy. This act split the tribe. Enough Osages supported the Confederacy to form a Confederate "Osage Battalion." Most Osages, however, seem to have favored the Union. The Confederate battalion was able to recruit only 200 men versus the promised 500. When the Second Indian Home Guard Regiment formed in Kansas in 1862, many Osages jointed that Federal organization instead. More dramatically, when a Confederate mounted detachment was discovered in Kansas in May of 1863, the Osages massacred the unit.

Despite the loyalty of the majority of the Osages, Kansas and the United States used the fact that tribe members had signed the Confederate treaty to disadvantage the tribe after the war. The Osages were forced to sell their Kansas reservation to the government and use the proceeds to purchase marginal land in the Cherokee Outlet in present-Oklahoma. The reservation proved the least arable in Oklahoma, and half of the nation died there in the first years of settlement. The Oklahoma reservation today has the unusual status of being simultaneously an Oklahoma county—Osage County—and the only Indian reservation technically surviving in Oklahoma.

C. *The Pawnees*—During the Civil War, the Pawnees occupied a reservation in south central Nebraska. In mid-1864, Lakotas and Cheyennes began a series of destructive raids against way stations on the Nebraska and Wyoming sections of the Oregon Trail. In August, a raiding party of Lakotas and their allies struck a combined train of freight and emigrant wagons near Plum Creek, near the western boundary of the Pawnee Reservation. Union Brig. Gen. Samuel R. Curtis recommended that Joseph McFadden and Frank North, who had both worked as clerks at the Pawnee Agency, recruit a company of Pawnee scouts to combat raiding Lakotas and Cheyennes. The Pawnees were traditional enemies of the Lakotas, and many were in need of employment. The first recruitment and use of Pawnees in the field was ineffectual. In the fall of 1864, North organized a new company, and it was sworn in as a Nebraska state volunteer company. It took the field shortly after the end of the Civil War in 1865 and immediately gained a reputation for hard fighting in Brig. Gen. Patrick E. Connor's Powder River Campaign. After it grew to became a battalion attached to the U.S. Army in 1867, North's Pawnee Scouts became the most famous Indian auxiliary unit of the Indian wars. It might be noted that Union state volunteers actually fought two skirmishes *against* Poncas during the Civil War.

D. *The Winnebagoes*—Few Indians in the United States were so frequently and casually forced to resettle and so badly used as the Winnebagoes. Between 1840 and 1865, the nation was removed westward five times, suffering a loss of 700 lives in the process. At the time of the Dakota or "Minnesota Sioux" conflict, the Winnebagoes were living in their second home in Minnesota. They were in the process of being exiled to Dakota Territory and were desperately poor when some of them were recruited in 1863 and 1864 as army scouts by the Yankton Sioux Indian agent. In this capacity the Winnebagoes accompanied Brig. Gen. Alfred Sully on his 1864 punitive expedition against the Dakotas and Lakotas in what is now western North Dakota. In addition to scouting, the Winnebagoes several times launched their own forays against the Dakotas.

Any hopes the Winnebagoes had that they would be rewarded for their service were soon dashed. As the Civil War ground to a conclusion, the nation was removed still again, this time to Nebraska. Still impoverished, Winnebagoes again hired out with the army and fought alongside North's Pawnee Scouts (above) in the postwar conflicts on the Northern Plains. The income as scouts was badly needed, for it would take them another twenty years to collect the pay they were owed from the Sully expedition.

IV. Indian Soldiers and Battles in the Indian Territory

The Confederate alliance treaties negotiated by Albert Pike gave the Confederacy the upper hand in the [Oklahoma] Indian Territory in 1861. Though the Confederacy only called for and authorized three Indian Territory regiments, four were quickly organized. (The Cherokee, Chickasaw, Choctaw, Creek, and Seminole units are described more specifically in the discussion of the Five Tribes above.) Out of an estimated prewar population of 65,000 persons, the Indian Territory provided at least 5,000 soldiers for the Confederacy and perhaps thousands more. These men were enrolled in a total of eight identifiable battalions (most if not all under five companies) and eleven regiments. As was typical of Civil War organizations, many of these were not recruited to regulation strength; also the companies of different regiments and battalions were occasionally broken up and transferred to new organizations. From 1863 to 1865, the two principal Cherokee regiments were the nucleus of one Indian brigade and the Chickasaw and Choctaw Cavalry Regiment the nucleus of another. The two Creek regiments were most often brigaded with the Cherokees, while the Osage and Seminole battalions were associated with several different commands. Both Indian brigades were often supplemented with Texas cavalry units. Confederate hopes for a third Indian brigade were never realized.

Most Confederate Indians were either in cavalry units or mounted infantry units; Western Confederate Indians, like their white counterparts, tended to favor mounted service. Confederate Indians generally fought alongside Texas cavalrymen, and the similarity in their loose, frontier fashion of fighting was often noted. The Indians were often described as proceeding into battle with "war whoops" by white observers. However, this did not particularly differentiate them from white Confederates who entered combat with "rebel yells." It was also sometimes charged that Confederate Indians were distinguished by the practice of scalping. However, the only well documented instance of scalping involved fewer than ten such acts in an early battle of the war at Pea Ridge, Arkansas, in 1862. [For the latest information about this incident, see *JIW*, Vol. 1, No. 3, pp. 115-125.] Nor was scalping unique to the Indians, as it was practiced by Texans as a form of body counting in frontier warfare with the Comanches. The single practice which anecdotal evidence suggests was perhaps more common among Indian soldiers than whites was the killing of enemy wounded and prisoners.

Officially, 3,530 men from the nations of the Indian Territory joined Union regiments. Many recruits came from the 5,000 Creeks and 1,700 Seminoles who somehow escaped alive from the Indian Territory while following Chief Opothleyahola in late 1861. Others came from Drew's Confederate Cherokee Regiment, which deserted en masse during 1861 and 1862. Still more soldiers were recruited from among Cherokee refugees who fled the wrath of Confederate Cherokees after the first Union expedition into Indian Territory was withdrawn in the summer of 1862. The exact number of recruits from the territory is difficult to determine. Some Indian Territory Indians joined white Kansas regiments while refugees in that state. Also, there were Union Delawares, Kickapoos, Osages, Quapaws, and Senecas in both Kansas and the Leased District, making it difficult to tell sometimes whether unit members were from Kansas or the Indian Territory. Most troops of Indian Territory were enrolled in three Indian Home Guard Regiments organized in southern Kansas. Unlike the case with the Confederate Indian regiments, white officers were assigned to each Union unit.

Initially, the creation of the three regiments had a humanitarian as well as a military objective. The United States commissioner of Indian Affairs, William Dole, learned in January 1862 that there were approximately 6,000 Indian Territory refugees homeless and starving in Kansas. He believed that a large force of Indian recruits could recover the Cherokee, Creek, and Seminole reservations. This would permit many Indian families to return home and plant that year, while at the same time driving Indian allies of the Confederacy farther from Kansas. The plan was approved in March by the War Department, and in May by the new commander of the Department of Kansas, Brig. Gen. James G. Blunt.

The First Kansas Indian Home Guard Regiment was organized in May of 1862 and was composed primarily of recruits from among Opothleyahola's Creek and Seminole followers. The Second Kansas Indian Home Guard Regiment, led by Colonel John Ritchie, was organized in June and July. It was made up of members of many different Indian nations, including Delawares, Kickapoos, Osages, Senecas, and Shawnees as well as more Creeks and Seminoles. There was insufficient time to recruit more Indian regiments and remain on schedule for the proposed expedition south, so the Ninth and Tenth Kansas cavalry regiments accompanied the two Indian regiments as they moved towards the Indian Territory. The resulting brigade was led by Colonel William Weer of the Tenth Kansas Infantry Regiment. Shortly after crossing into Indian Territory, the expedition on July 3 surprised a Confederate force of Missourians and Cherokees at Locust Grove. This marked the first occasion during the war of enrolled Union Indians fighting enrolled Confederate Indians. A number of the men of Drew's Confederate Cherokee regiment deserted to the Second Kansas Indian regiment at the end of the engagement. The column seemed sure of success when it captured Tahlequah, the Cherokee capital, on July 16 and the key post of Fort Gibson on July 18. However, a bizarre quarrel broke out between Weer and his second in command, who replaced Weer and recalled the expedition.

A third Indian regiment, to be led by Colonel William A. Phillips, was being organized while the other two were in the field. A fourth regiment was begun but never completed. After the first and second regiments returned home, the three Union Indian units were redesignated as United States (versus Kansas) volunteer regiments. When brigaded together and supplemented by Kansas state regiments, the resulting organization would often be known as the "Union Indian Brigade." General Blunt utilized the brigade in fighting in Missouri, Arkansas, and the Indian Territory in the latter part of 1862. In April of 1863, Blunt established his departmental headquarters at Fort Gibson, the most important position in the Indian Territory. It was also a point from which his forces could take part in the multi-theater wave of offensives the United States had planned for the spring of 1863. The Confederates west of the Mississippi River were goaded to respond to Blunt's presence so far south. Brig. Gen. Douglas H. Cooper pulled together all of the supplies and men he could from across his Confederate Department of the Indian Territory, until he had assembled a force of 6,000 soldiers. He was to be reinforced from western Arkansas by the 3,000 troops of Brig. Gen. William L. Cabell.

In response to Cooper's effort, Blunt had additional troops and supplies rushed toward Fort Gibson from the Federal base at Fort Scott, Kansas. On July 1 and 2, 1863, Stand Watie's Confederate Indian brigade attempted to halt and destroy a train of 200 wagons at the crossing of Cabin Creek on the Military Road. The wagon escort, primarily the First Kansas Colored Infantry Regiment, pushed the Confederates aside. Federal forces at Fort Gibson were then resupplied in preparation for Blunt's offensive. Blunt, however, soon learned of the anticipated juncture of Cooper's and Cabell's troops. If it came about, he would have only 3,000 Federals in the field to face 9,000 Confederates. Blunt decided to attack Cooper's Confederates before Cabell's men could arrive from Arkansas.

Blunt's Kansans, Wisconsins, Coloradans, and Indians encountered Cooper's Texas and Indian brigades on the Texas Road north of Elk Creek and the Confederate supply depot at Honey Springs. The fighting reached its peak during a firefight near the center of the lines, where the First Kansas Colored Infantry confronted the Twentieth and Twenty-ninth Texas cavalry regiments. Part of the Second Indian Home Guard Regiment inadvertently moved into the line of fire between the black troops and the Texans. When the Indians were ordered to fall back into position, the Texans overheard the command and mistook it for an order to withdraw from the field. The Confederates immediately pressed to within seventy-five feet of the First Kansas, only to be met twice with a volley of rifle fire at point blank range. The regimental flag of one of the Texas regiments fell three times, and the third time it was seized by soldiers from the Second Indian Home Guard. Meanwhile, Cooper decided to retreat when he learned that his left flank was in danger and that much of his gunpowder was damp or defective. He pulled his brigades back across Elk Creek. The Choctaw and Chickasaw Regiment and a token force of Texas cavalry valiantly covered the Confederate retreat. The Battle of Honey Springs was the largest battle in the Indian Territory. A greater number of Indians were engaged in it than in any other battle in North American history.

Honey Springs was also the climactic battle of the war in Indian Territory. Blunt was soon reinforced and proceeded to scatter the Confederates in the territory. Six weeks after the battle, he captured Fort Smith, the Confederate base for western Arkansas. In the process, he tied up Confederate forces that could have assisted in the defense of Little Rock. That city, the capital of Arkansas, fell scarcely a week later. For the duration of the war there would be but a single large Confederate operation in the West that managed to proceed north of the Arkansas River. This effort was Maj. Gen. Sterling Price's disastrous Missouri expedition of September and October, 1864, which was essentially a large-scale cavalry raid.

In conjunction with Price's expedition, Watie's Confederate Indian brigade and Brig. Gen. Richard M. Gano's Texas brigade were authorized to carry out a raid on a train of 200 supply wagons bound for Fort Gibson. The attack at the Cabin Creek crossing on September 19, 1864, was a complete success. The raid netted Watie and Gano 130 wagons of badly needed rations and materials and deprived the Union Army of the Frontier of 1.5 million dollars worth of supplies. But while the results provided temporary encouragement for the Confederates of Indian Territory, the outcome did the Federals no irreparable harm. The war was already lost, and the Battle of Second Cabin Creek would be the last notable military event in Indian Territory. [For a detailed examination of this action, see "Stand Watie and the Battles of First and Second Cabin Creek," by Palmer Boeger, *JIW*, Vol. 1, no. 3, pp. 45-68.]

When the Union and Confederate Indian veterans returned home, they found themselves in the most savaged area within the boundaries of the United States. In the words of the old W.P.A. guide to Oklahoma, "No part of the South or the border region where the actual fighting took place suffered losses more horrible than those of the Indian Territory." Hundreds of Indian soldiers and perhaps thousands of Indian civilians were dead. A census of Union Cherokees midway through the war showed that a third of their women had already become widows and a quarter of the Cherokee children orphans. The percentages were likely typical of Confederate Cherokees and of other Indian nations as well. Virtually all of the mills and perhaps the majority of farm structures in the Indian Territory were destroyed. There was scarcely a cow or hog left in the entire territory, and most fields had not yielded a crop in three years. As many as 18,000 Cherokee, Chickasaw, Creek, and Seminole and Leased District refugees in Texas had to return home to reservations stripped bare. Perhaps as many as 17,000 Union and neutral Cherokees, Creeks, and Leased District Indians sheltering in Kansas and northeastern Oklahoma faced the same prospects.

V. Eastern Indian Peoples Recruited as Troops, Scouts, and Auxiliaries During the Civil War

Indians east of the Mississippi River also felt they had several good reasons to participate as soldiers and auxiliaries in a war not their own. These included: a) the hope of avoiding tribal removal westward; b) the hope of securing recognition of tribal government or of reservation boundaries; c) economic dependence; and d) the prospect of revenge upon Southern advocates of racism and Indian removal. The hope of avoiding exile to reservations west of the Mississippi River was by far the most important factor in eastern Indian military service. Eastern Indians felt strongly motivated to try to win the favor of United States or Confederate officials who might intervene for them against the tide of Indian removal.

A. New York and Great Lakes States Indians

In central New York and western Wisconsin, bands of the once powerful Six Nations or "Iroquois Confederacy" found possession of their reservations seriously jeopardized by illegal land sales and land auctions. Their solution was in part to enlist in Union volunteer regiments and hope that the United States government would intervene and grant formal recognition of their reservation status and boundaries. Some of the Oneida nation enlisted in the Fourteenth Wisconsin Infantry Regiment. Members of the Tuscarora and Seneca Nations in New York attempted to enroll early on, but the racism of state authorities ran so deep that they were rejected. Officials finally relented when the state's manpower supply ran low by the summer of 1862, and the Tuscarora and

Seneca enlisted in the One Hundred and Thirty-second New York Infantry and later the Fourteenth New York Heavy Artillery. One particularly prominent Seneca, the sachem and spokesman Ely Parker, would serve as General Ulysses S. Grant's military secretary.

In Michigan and Wisconsin, the pressure for removal of tribes to Indian Territory was almost as great as the assault in Kansas. Several bands of Great Lakes Indians hoped that their loyalty to the Union would be rewarded with the opportunity to renegotiate their treaties on a more favorable and secure basis. As a result, some Ottawas and Ojibwas joined the First Michigan Sharpshooter Regiment—there was some preference among eastern Indians for duty as sharpshooters just as there was a preference for mounted service among western Indians. Several Ottawas and Ojibwas would become famous for their marksmanship during the siege of Vicksburg. Historian Laurence Hauptman has also found that small numbers of impoverished New England Indians, underemployed from the decline of the whaling industry, joined United States Colored Troop regiments.

B. Tidewater and Piedmont Region Indians

The Indians of coastal and lowland Virginia, North Carolina, and South Carolina were perhaps the most victimized of any in the eastern United States. These states possessed deep-rooted fears of unfree blacks revolting and of free blacks achieving social and economic independence. Because these states often classified Indians as "free persons of color," Indians there were subjected to the paranoia with which many whites viewed free blacks or potential freedom fighters. During the course of the war, North and South Carolina subjected most of the Indians within their borders to conscription as forced labor for the war effort. In Virginia, the Pamunkeys retaliated. As the 1862 Peninsula campaign approached Richmond, local Pamunkeys assisted the Federals as scouts and as "river pirates" on the James and York rivers. In North Carolina, the multi-ethnic Lumbees operated out of the coastal swamps as Union partisans or guerrillas. They would long be treated as "outlaws" as a consequence. Only one group of lowland Indians allied itself with the Confederacy, the Catawbas of the Piedmont region of South Carolina. This group was very small. The members were also in a very precarious state, having been deprived of their land by an illegal South Carolina treaty in 1840. The Catawbas survived by catching slaves for plantation owners and cooperating with their neighbors in any other way possible. As a result, they were helplessly dependent upon the goodwill of white South Carolinians by the time of the Civil War. When the war began, the few Catawba men—only fifty-five by 1861—began to enroll in the Fifth, Twelfth, and Seventh South Carolina infantry regiments. As was the case with most Civil War Indians, the Catawba's military service got them little benefit. The band was still attempting to secure state recognition and land compensation in 1993 when the federal government finally intervened. The Lumbees, on the other hand, remain the country's largest group of Indian descent (over 40,000 members) still without national or state recognition.

C. The Eastern Band Cherokees

The largest number of eastern Indians in enrolled military service were eastern band Cherokees. These were descendants of the approximately 1,000 Cherokees who had managed to escape removal to the western Indian Territory via the "Trail of Tears" of 1838-1839. Many of these Cherokees, the "Oconaluftee Citizen Band" or Quallatown Band of North Carolina, had lived outside of the eastern Cherokee reservation at the time of removal. Others had been reservation Indians who had fled into the Great Smoky Mountains to escape removal. All such Cherokee living in the East pinned their hopes upon an 1848 Congressional resolution recognizing their right to remain in any state that would grant them status as permanent residents. Unfortunately, the states that

Thomas's Legion, a postwar image.

Thomas's Confederate Legion

all remnant Cherokees lived in (Georgia, Tennessee, and North Carolina) had been the very Southern states that had clamored for their removal. At the time of the Civil War, no state had granted them sanctuary. North Carolina had done them a further injury by classifying them as "free persons of color," which subjected them to taxation while depriving them of the right to vote or own property.

The eastern Cherokees' rather ironic decision to ally themselves with the Confederacy in 1861 was largely due to the charismatic leadership of an adopted white member of the band, William Holland Thomas. Thomas had been raised by a Oconoluftee elder and had become the band's unofficial spokesman in the North Carolina and national capitals. He also held the deeds to much of the Cherokees land on behalf of the band as the Cherokees were not permitted to hold title. Thomas convinced many eastern Cherokee that the "states's rights" philosophy of the Confederate states might somehow be converted into an argument for Cherokee autonomy. In addition, Thomas argued, the state of North Carolina might develop sufficient appreciation for Cherokee military service that it would recognize resident and/or reservation status for the eastern band.

As a result of Thomas's persuasion, the eastern Cherokee in 1861 enrolled in a Cherokee military company. This was expanded and joined to several companies of Tennessee and North Carolina volunteers. By October of 1862, the organization was composed of two Indian and six white companies and was designated as the Sixty-ninth North Carolina infantry, or "Thomas's Legion of Indians and Highlanders." In 1863, the two Cherokee companies were detached but were later joined with two additional companies to form the four company, 300-350 man Cherokee battalion. This battalion represented almost all of the adult males of the Quallatown band. During the war, the eastern Cherokee companies guarded mountain passes and served as a deterrent against the activities of the many Union sympathizers in the Appalachian highlands.

As Thomas hoped, shortly after the war (1866) North Carolina recognized the Cherokees' residency rights. At about the same time, the United States finally met its obligations under two early nineteenth century treaties and allocated money to protect the debt-ridden Thomas's land titles. Ironically, the largest eastern Indian population disloyal to the United States was the sole Indian nation to be significantly rewarded for its role in the Civil War.

BIBLIOGRAPHIC INFORMATION

Two published sets of primary sources are essential in researching the role and conflicts of American Indians in the period of the American Civil War. One is the "Bible" of Civil War scholars, the seventy-volume, one hundred and twenty-eight part work *The War of the Rebellion: A Compilation of the Official Records of the Union and Confederate Armies* (Washington, D.C.: U.S. Government Printing Office, 1880-1901). The *Official Records* or *OR*, as it is commonly known, contains most of the known battle and campaign reports of the years 1861-1865, including those for Western states. The other important primary source is the two volume *Documents of American Indian Diplomacy: Treaties, Agreements, and Conventions, 1775-1979*, edited by Vine Deloria, Jr., and Raymond J. DeMallie (Norman: University of Oklahoma Press, 1999). This new publication contains the texts of all wartime Union and Confederate Indian treaties, including those contracted by Albert Pike.

Leroy H. Fischer is the most prolific historian with regard to the Indian Territory during the Civil War. His *The Civil War Era in Indian Territory* (Los Angeles: Lorin L. Morrison, 1976) is a basic book on the subject. An out-of-print work, Larry C. Rampp's *Civil War in the Indian Territory* (Austin: Presidial Press, 1975) contains some helpful maps of Indian Territory campaigns and battles. On the wartime division and rival regiments of the Cherokee people, Kenny A. Franks's *Stand Watie and the Agony of the Cherokee Nation* (Memphis: Memphis State University Press, 1979; out of print) is the most perceptive work so far. Frank Cunningham's *General Stand Watie's Confederate Indians* (1959; reprint, Norman: University of Oklahoma Press, 1998) provides factual information on the battles fought by Watie's "Cherokee brigade" but is otherwise superficial. For the best information on the even greater tragedy of the Creeks and the factors involved in Opothleyahola's flight, see Christine Schultz White and Benton R. White, *Now the Wolf Has Come: The Creek Nation in the Civil War* (College Station: Texas A & M Press, 1996). Regretfully little has been done on Union Indians from Indian Territory. This leaves an old work, *The Union Indian Brigade in the Civil War* by Wiley Britton (Kansas City: Franklin Hudson Publishing Company, 1922; out of print) as the most important secondary source on that subject.

Only the second chapter of Thomas W. Dunlay's *Wolves for the Blue Soldiers: Indian Scouts and Auxiliaries with the United States Army, 1860-1890* (Lincoln: University of Nebraska Press, 1982) deals with the recruitment of Indian auxiliaries for Western campaigns during the Civil War, but that makes Dunlay's book the standard on the subject. Laurence M. Hauptman's highly regarded *Between Two Fires: American Indians in the Civil War* (New York: Free Press, 1995) concerns the recruitment of

Indians in all theaters during the war, but is most valuable and original in its examination of the enlistment of east coast and Great Lakes Indians.

Thomas's Legion is the subject of Vernon Crow's *Storm in the Mountains: Thomas' Confederate Legion of Cherokee Indians and Mountaineers* (Cherokee, NC: Press of the Museum of the Cherokee Indian, 1982; out of print).

THE ASCENT OF THE
Cheyenne Dog Soldiers, 1838-1869

Richard S. Grimes

T he awesome Plains warriors were "armed to the teeth with revolvers and bows . . . proud, haughty, defiant as should become those who are to grant favors, not beg them."[1]

With these words, an Ohio reporter covering the critical negotiations at Medicine Lodge Creek in Kansas described the arrival of over 500 Cheyenne Dog Soldiers on October 27, 1867. Their proud arrival at the treaty grounds, some seventy miles south of Fort Larned, left a lasting impression on all of those who witnessed their grand entrance. As the Dog Soldiers came within sight of the camp, they gave chilling war cries and fired their rifles into the air. Their ponies whipped through the high weeds, and they brandished their feathered lances and rifles high over their heads as they rode into the lodge circles.

Henry M. Stanley, a young British journalist who later would gain world renown for his adventures in Africa, accompanied the United States Army to Medicine Lodge Creek as a war correspondent for the St. Louis *Daily Missouri Democrat*. He was as impressed with the entry of the Dog Soldiers as his fellow journalist. Stanley acknowledged that the "vaunted Kiowa, the terrible Comanche and the redoubtable Arapaho paled before the . . . Cheyenne, the Scourge of the Plains."[2] Billy Dixon, a scout and buffalo hunter, was in a state of awe as he watched "resplendent warriors, armed with all their equipment and adorned with all the regalia of battle [who] seemed to be rising out of the earth." He surmised that this militant posturing was an effective way to "create as profound an impression as possible, and inspire us deeply with their power."[3]

According to Stanley, the Dog Soldiers remained alert and imposing throughout the treaty negotiations: "Sitting astride their ponies, watching with fierce eyes every movement that is going on, their heads adorned with nodding plumes, their faces painted red, blue, black or yellow, they present in my mind the safe-guard of a nation, the forlorn hope of the Indians. In this band, haughty and obstinate, are to be found the best representative of the American aboriginal, who are still extant." He concluded that the Dog Soldiers were "[M]odern Spartans, who knew how to die but not to be led captive."[4]

The treaty talks between the Southern Plains Indian nations and the United States began at the camp of the federal commissioners. Thousands of Southern Cheyenne, Southern Arapahoes, Comanches, Kiowas, and Kiowa-Apaches met with the government representatives to discuss a treaty that would restrict Indian movement north of the Arkansas River. In return, whites would be forbidden from hunting south of the Arkansas. The reserved area would be protected as the exclusive domain of the Indians for as long as bison herds roamed on the southern Plains. There were both positive and negative aspects to this treaty. However, even had the treaty totally favored the Indians' interests, the Cheyenne present would have refrained from immediately signing. Only 150 Cheyenne were in attendance, mostly chiefs. The majority of the Southern Cheyenne remained camped farther to the west on the Cimarron River. In this camp were the Dog Soldiers, the military elite of the Cheyenne nation [*Tsistsistas*]. The Cheyenne leaders at Medicine Lodge Creek would not sign the treaty until the Dog Soldiers considered the matter and gave their approval.[5]

The treaty was ratified by the Cheyenne only when the Dog Soldier leaders came forward to sign their names. Journalistic accounts concerning the Dog Soldiers may have been embellished with a dramatic and romantic flair, but they illustrated the vivid impressions left upon whites who witnessed the intimidating presence of these Cheyenne warriors. Significantly, the Dog Soldiers displayed what Cheyenne considered to be the ultimate expression of their manhood and tribal identity. It was only fitting that at the Medicine Lodge talks the members of this fraternal society asserted their martial potency to the alien people who were threatening Cheyenne existence. But the warriors represented more than simply a means of defense of the Cheyenne nation. The Dog Soldiers had transcended their original responsibility and duty as a soldier society and risen to a position of military and political dominance among the Cheyenne people.

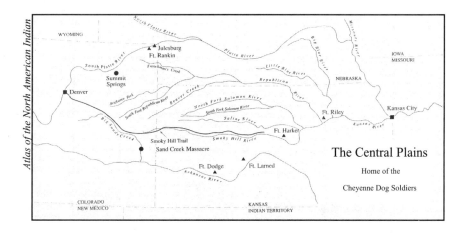

The Cheyenne lived in an area penetrated by wandering war parties of enemy nations and occupied by swift and dangerous game. A selfish hunter who proceeded on his own during a communal hunt risked chasing away a bison herd, thus jeopardizing the food supply of an entire village. There also had to be coordination between individuals and the military societies on camp duty to order to successfully conduct war. In addition, there was a perceived necessity to have camps policed to insure compliance with Cheyenne demands for self-control. Among the Cheyenne, as in most Plains nations, there was a need for "authoritative officialdom," for a sanctioned, authoritative body or bodies which could "hold in check" unrestrained members, but would do so without being too coercive or dictatorial.[6] Military societies. fraternal warrior clubs, were sanctioned by Cheyenne governmental structure to counter the actions of individuals who threatened the communal welfare of the Cheyenne people.

The power and necessity of military societies was especially evident when, in times of major armed conflicts, they forbade the individualistic pursuit of glory. All Cheyenne military action had to be sanctioned by war leaders. Despite this, many young men from different societies would try to leave and go out on independent excursions against the enemy. For this reason, the soldier societies would conduct a police watch. It was quite an accomplishment for a warrior to avoid detection and and escape camp.

One example of such security enforcement occurred in June of 1876, when some some Cheyenne joined the Lakota Sioux on the Little Bighorn to form a massive village. The war leaders of the Cheyenne soldier societies there were willing to wait and see if the white soldiers attacked them. These authorities ordered the young Cheyenne men to stay put and "leave the soldiers alone unless they attack us." The military societies worked day and night patrolling the Little Bighorn on both banks to make sure that young men did not creep out to be the first to fight the approaching cavalrymen.[7] This was an example of a case where insistence on the welfare of the whole people could supersede the desire of "eager young men" seeking to obtain status.

The role of the soldier societies is to this day honored in Cheyenne oral history and folklore. According to tradition, in the distant past bands of Cheyenne people lived in disorder and chaos. There was chronic theft and murder among members. To find a solution to these social problems, Sweet Medicine, the Cheyenne's central cultural hero, ventured into the heart of the Black Hills country. When he reached the sacred mountain known by Cheyenne as Noahvose (today's Bear Butte, South Dakota), he encountered a group of old men and old women. These elders instructed Sweet Medicine on how to solve the problem of Cheyenne anarchy. He was told to implement "good government" by forming a council of forty-four chiefs and by organizing military societies to maintain a "good system of police and military protection."[8] Both Cheyenne civil councils and Cheyenne military organizations were, as the story suggests, structured on the basis of tradition and protocol.

There were eventually six military societies: the Kit-Fox Men (*Woksihitaneo*); Red Shields (*Mahohivas*); Crazy Dogs (*Hotamimasaw*); Crooked Lance Society (*Himoiyoqis*), known by the ethnohistorian George Grinnell as the Elks; Bowstring Men *(Himatanohis);* Wolf Warriors *(Konianutqio)*; and the Dog Men or Dog Soldiers *(Hotamitaneo).* Though this list contains seven names, many scholars accept the view of George Bird Grinnell and his chief informant George Bent that the Bowstring Men and Wolf Warriors were the same society. The Bowstrings were Southern Cheyenne while the Crazy Dogs were found exclusively among the Northern Cheyenne. The most militant and elite society was that of the Dog Soldiers. Though the last group to emerge, it became the most important, rising to unique prominence and power. The ascension of this society by the mid-1850s demonstrated the ability of the Cheyenne to respond to the national crisis created when United States citizens poured into the Cheyenne homeland.[9] The Dog Soldiers evolved into a political and military juggernaut in response to the assault.

Soldier societies provided martial training, socialization, and preservation of tradition among the men who joined the groups. Each Cheyenne fraternal organization had its sacred symbols, decorations, dances, and songs. This made members of each club different from those of other groups and distinct from Cheyenne society as a whole. Red Shield soldiers carried red shields that had the tail of a bison hanging from the base.[10] Wolf Soldiers were well known for both their military prowess and also for their elaborate social gatherings, which were complete with "noisy songs . . . effusive dances and the sparkling and varied colors of their outfits."[11]

Crooked Lance society members wrapped their lances in otter skins, while each member of the Dog Soldiers wore on his chest a whistle made of the bone of a bird. Four of the bravest Dog Soldiers were chosen to wear sashes of tanned skins called "dog ropes" into battle. Attached to each dog rope was a picket pin [used to tether horses]. The pin was driven into the ground as a mark of resolve in combat. When a Dog Soldier was staked to the ground in order to cover the retreat of his companions, he was required to remain there even if death was the consequence. The Dog Man could pull the pin from the ground only if his companions reached safety or another Dog Soldier released him from his duty.[12]

The societies illustrated the "competitive nature of [Indian] warfare." A fierce contest existed between the various Cheyenne military organizations. Each society formed its own war parties and tried to "exceed the military accomplishments of rival societies."[13] Wooden Leg, who as a seventeen-year-

"White Horse Battles the Delawares." This Cheyenne pictograph, drawn by a Dog Soldier named White Horse, shows him fighting two Delaware Indians.

Cheyenne Dog Soldiers: A Ledgerbook History of Coups and Combat

old warrior helped to defeat Lt. Col. George Armstrong Custer's command at the Little Bighorn, recalled that "the warrior societies competed with each other for effectiveness" in war and in status within the community. If an enemy party was small in number, soldier leaders selected only a few certain members of a society to do the fighting. "If this appointed segment of our fighters did well they were acclaimed. If they did not do well, especially if other warriors had to go to their assistance, the original combatants were discredited."[14]

Theoretically, the societies were to maintain order without resorting to crushing a person's individualism through excessive punishment. However, on many occasions the members resorted to extreme measures to maintain discipline. Colonel Richard Dodge observed the duties of the Dog Soldiers when it was their turn to police a camp. The colonel noted that "they supply the guards for the camp, designate the hunting parties and the ground they are to work over . . . and they select the keen-eyed hunters who are to go in advance. A violation of the Dog-Soldiers rules is at once met by a sound beating."[15]

In one instance, six Cheyenne were sent to locate a Pawnee camp that was to be attacked. The soldier society leading the raid instructed the scouts to kill any enemy found along the way who might alert the Pawnee camp of the impending attack. The Cheyenne "wolves" (i.e., scouts) came across one Pawnee who stood his ground, wounded one Cheyenne, and drove the rest away. As they returning to the main camp, the wolves decided not to tell the members of their soldier society that they had been beaten by one Pawnee. A wounded scout named Wolf Mule, however, "unfolded under questioning" by members of the society and confessed. The soldiers whipped the other scouts with pony quirts, but they did not harm the informer.[16]

While violations were generally at the individual level, there were occasions when entire bodies were confronted by the soldiers. Cheyenne bands were occasionally summoned by important leaders to meet at a central location in preparation for war or a communal hunt. Some bands would occasionally dawdle on the way. A band of Cheyenne once refused to move camp quickly to answer a summons. The group was in a safe area with ample game so the members decided to enjoy the surroundings before moving on to the main tribal location. After a few days, they were "suddenly pounced upon by an overwhelming force of dog-soldiers." The soldiers went directly to the women and "ordered [the women] to pack at once." Those who did not move quickly were "beaten with a rod." Within hours the camp was packed and the women and children, who bore the duty of packing, followed the soldiers to the new location. The "lovers, husbands, and fathers could do nothing but sullenly follow." The Dog Men thwarted this temporary rebellion, the guilty suffered humiliation in front of the rest of the tribe, and Cheyenne order and Dog Soldier authority were reestablished.[17]

As the examples above indicate, the Dog Soldiers or *Hotamitaneo* asserted their dominance in many areas. They and the members of the other soldiers clubs maintained order in both the civil and the military spheres of Cheyenne life. However, there had been traditional distinctions between civil and military authority among the Cheyenne. This tradition is reflected in the story of Sweet Medicine's creating a council of forty-four chiefs that was distinct from the soldier societies. The ascension of the Dog Soldiers marked a breakdown of the separation between the civil and military elements of Cheyenne society.

The Dog Soldiers evolved into a political and military power as United States citizens poured into the Cheyenne homeland in the mid-1800s. As was their right in times of conflict, the military societies gained more control over their nation since its total mobilization was required to counter the assault. As the cultural and military crisis deepened, the soldier societies responded by becoming more assertive. As their influence increased, the societies at times became arbitrary and dictatorial in their relationship with civil leadership and the community. The Dog Soldiers in particular came to exercise enormous influence and power.

Yet the rise of the Dog Soldiers was not originally inspired by some momentous event in Cheyenne history. Instead, their ascent began with a sordid incident years earlier that had freed them from many of the constraints of Cheyenne tradition and protocol. Early in the winter of 1838, the Dog Soldier leader Porcupine Bear and a few of his warriors were traveling from camp to camp to recruit other societies to join them in a raid against the Kiowas. One village, located on the South Platte River in Wyoming, had just obtained whiskey from the American Fur Company post at Fort William (the future Fort Laramie). According to Grenville Dodge, the "whole camp went to drinking that night." Porcupine Bear and his men became drunk, and during the celebration, his two cousins Little Creek and Around became embroiled in a brawl. Around, getting beaten, begged Porcupine Bear to help him.

Porcupine Bear paid no attention. He sat alone in a corner of the lodge, singing to himself in a low voice. He was very drunk and was singing Dog Soldier songs. Presently Little Creek rolled on top of Around and, drawing his knife, raised his arm to strike, but at that moment Porcupine Bear leaped up in a sudden rage; and, springing upon Little Creek, he wrenched the knife from his hand and stabbed him two or three times. He then forced the knife into Around's hand and, standing over him, compelled him to finish Little Creek.[18]

For this crime, Porcupine Bear and his followers were deemed outlaws by the tribe. They were forbidden to camp with other Cheyenne and banned from all national functions. Ostracized from society, Porcupine Bear and his men could only set up their lodges "near the village—a mile or two from it."[19] The Dog Soldier Society in general "was also disgraced," and it was relieved of any future police responsibility.[20] Porcupine Bear and his warriors still kept contact with other Cheyenne camps and fought on their behalf. In a battle at Wolf Creek with the Comanches and Kiowas, his men counted first coup, and Porcupine Bear singularly killed twelve Kiowas. However, the Dog Men were still outlaws and could not accorded any recognized honors of war.[21]

This alienation from the main camp, instead of chastening the warriors, led to the Dog Soldiers' independence. Instead of being under the traditional band chiefs, the Dog Soldiers were now governed by their own band chiefs, all of whom were war leaders. Men who became Dog Soldiers did so with the understanding that they would have to move their families and take up full-time residency among the Dogs. John H. Moore has described this development as an "extraordinary feature [that] endowed the Dog society with a unique cohesiveness and gave rise to [the] . . . possibilities of governmental formation."[22] The distinction between being a military society and being a band became blurred as the Dog Soldiers became a separate division of the Cheyenne people.

Despite their alienation, the defiant and elite Dog Soldiers had no difficulty attracting young warriors. Petersen notes in the thoughtful study of Cheyenne military societies that after the banishment, recruitment into the society "snowballed until it comprised half of the fighting force of the tribe."[23] The Dog Soldiers lured the most militant of warriors into their ranks, for their members would not give an inch to accommodate whites because they offered an alternative to the failed peace policies of civil leaders who were unable to prevent encroachment on their territory.

By the 1850s, the Cheyenne, like most Plains tribes, were entering a state of national crisis. A few farsighted whites predicted the coming catastrophe awaiting tribes, such as the Cheyenne. Thomas "Broken Hand" Fitzpatrick was a veteran plains man who represented the Cheyenne and Arapaho as their agent. He became deeply concerned for the welfare of these people when he noticed the thinning out of the massive southern bison herds. In 1853 Fitzpatrick addressed the Bureau of Indian Affairs on the severity of the situation. He claimed that as "startling as it may appear . . . the Cheyenne and Arapahoes, and many of the Sioux, are actually in a starving state." The agent noted the drastic decrease in bison counts and the conditions of the Cheyenne who were "in abject want of food half the year."[24]

Other warnings came from Indian trader William Bent. He contacted the bureau in 1859, stressing the danger of allowing gold seekers to migrate into the mountain regions of Colorado. Bent believed that the intruders were disrupting the winter domain of the Cheyenne. "A smothered passion for revenge agitates these Indians," warned Bent, "perpetually fomented by the failure [to find] food, the encircling encroachments of the white population, and the exasperating sense of decay and impending extinction with which they are surrounded."[25]

John Moore has analyzed the rise of the Dog Soldiers as part of a "military imperative" that existed among the Cheyenne in the 1860s and 1870s. The Dog Men represented a "reorganization of Cheyenne society, a geographical movement, and . . . a strong position on a political question" in a disastrously changing world.[26] The Dog Soldiers attracted all those who were unequivocally hostile to the "encroachments" and who chose war as the means to repulse this invasion of Indian country.

As the Dog Soldiers increased in members, they established a new domain for themselves. Dog Soldiers roamed east of the other Cheyenne bands, residing near the headwaters of the Republican and Smoky Hill between the Platte and Arkansas Rivers. In this region they camped and intermarried with Republican River Brule and Oglala Lakotas. By the 1860s, bands of Lakota warriors and Cheyenne Dog Soldiers became fused into a single unit.[27] The "restless and warlike elements" of Brule and Oglala Lakotas were attracted by the defiant and obstinate nature of the Dog Soldiers, and vice versa.[28] Together, the Cheyenne, their Arapaho associates, and the Lakotas would often form an informal alliance in the 1860s and 1870s to bar Euro-American settlement and fight the United States military on the central and northern Plains. Cheyenne warriors also rode with Arapahoes, Kiowas, and Comanches on the southern Plains to resist the intrusion of whites into their hunting grounds there as well.

While most Cheyenne continued to honor the the civil chiefs for their wisdom and senior standing in society, young warriors gravitated toward militant factions such as the Dog Soldiers, for these were "men of direct action."

They preferred the leaders of the *Hotamitaneo* over those leaders who advocated peace, even though there was still much sentiment for it among both the Northern and Southern Cheyenne.[29] Elbridge Gerry, a rancher and a representative of the United States Commissioner of Indian Affairs who was friendly towards the Cheyenne, believed that increasing numbers of warriors "were determined to sweep the Platte and the country as far as they could" of settlers. He noted that the civil leaders were becoming increasingly powerless, for the "young men could not be controlled."[30] Gerry witnessed an unusual example of the "young men's" militancy in 1863. In that year the Dog Soldiers "forbade" one of their own principal leaders, Bull Bear, from attending a Southern Cheyenne treaty council with Gerry. The Dog Soldiers feared that Bull Bear might be swayed by the influence of the peace chiefs there. They were determined to prevent the cession of more of the Republican River and Smoky Hill River country through the signing of another disastrous treaty like that made at Fort Wise, Colorado, two years earlier.[31]

Many observers during this time believed that the Dog Soldiers had taken control of the Southern Cheyenne. While the civil chiefs attempted to carry out their traditional authority, white officials steadily recognized the *Hotamitaneo* as the main source of tribal power. Territorial Governor John Evans of Colorado in 1865 testified to Congress that the Dog Soldiers "took the control of the tribe mainly out of the hands of the chiefs." Civil chiefs such as Black Kettle, White Antelope and Spotted Horse could not restrain the Dogs from warrior activity, even after the council of chiefs had agreed upon peace, for this "vigilance committee [i.e., the Dog Soldiers] . . . managed the tribe instead of the chiefs."[32] The army scout and interpreter Ben Clark maintained that the Dog Soldiers enjoyed superiority over the other Cheyenne bands. The Dog Soldiers, because of their numerical strength and "prestige of their leaders . . . practically ruled the tribe . . . . When the Dog Soldiers wanted war the whole tribe warred."[33]

George Bent, the son of trader William Bent and Owl Woman, his Cheyenne wife, also contended that the Dog Soldiers were "wild and reckless" and hard to control.[34] However, he credited them with being excellent raiders and premier warriors. During the 1860s, the Dog Soldiers struck rail stations, wagon trains, and settlements and temporarily held off further expansion into Cheyenne country. Unfortunately, because of the Dog Soldiers activities (as well as those of other soldier societies), peaceful Cheyenne became the target of territorial militias and the American military. The most tragic case of this came with the slaughter of the peace chief Black Kettle's people at Sand Creek, Colorado, in November of 1864.

The destruction of Black Kettle's village had two significant impacts on Cheyenne warfare. First, other warrior societies than the Dog Soldiers, such as the Elks, Kit Foxes, and Bowstrings became alienated from the civil chiefs and their peace efforts. They would increasingly ride out and fight as unrestricted autonomous bands.[35] Second, many Cheyenne became convinced that when fighting the United States they needed to be constantly prepared for war. In earlier decades, Cheyenne wars had usually been with other Plains peoples. These affairs were a seasonal activity. War parties generally fought in the warmer weather and ceased their martial activity during the winter months. But the surprise attack on the encampment at Sand Creek in the dead of winter changed all of this. In the words of a study by John H. Moore, "Cheyenne society was transformed onto a war footing," and thus military leaders came to the forefront of hierarchy.[36] The Dog Soldiers set a trend of soldier societies maintaining a "permanent residence" in camp rather than being appointed by civil leadership on a seasonal basis. Military leaders were now firmly in control of the Cheyenne hierarchy.[37]

Warriors who fought as members or associates of the Dog Soldiers were the Cheyenne nation's hope of repelling invasion. One such warrior was Roman Nose (Woo-Kay-Nay or "Arched Nose"). Roman Nose was a Northern Cheyenne who had distinguished himself among his people to such a high degree that the United States military misidentified him as the chief of the Cheyenne nation. Roman Nose was not a chief at all, but an influential member of the Crooked Lance warrior society. He was considered to be a "superb specimen of Cheyenne manhood" and was known by George Bent, who was also a member of the society.[38] Bent describe Roman Nose as a "man of fine character, quiet and self-contained." At the same time, Roman Nose was a dangerous fighter who counted many coup and gained great prestige and high status in Cheyenne society. According to Bent, "All the Cheyenne, both men and women, held him in the highest esteem."[39]

Roman Nose established himself as a warrior following the Sand Creek Massacre. To avenge the deaths of the Indian women and children at Sand Creek, an allied force of Cheyenne, Arapahoes, and Lakotas began in the early part of 1865 to lay waste to 400 miles of settlement. They burned ranches, farms, and telegraph offices and drove off cattle. Denver was cut off from supplies and was virtually besieged.[40] Roman Nose had come south to participate in the raids and rode with the Dog Soldiers, leading retaliatory strikes along the North and South Platte rivers in the early part of 1865. The Dog Soldiers and Roman Nose's own followers created such destruction on the Smoky Hill Road that it disrupted travel through though Kansas to Colorado. The government demanded that the Cheyenne cease the raiding or face extermination.

A peace parley between the Dog Soldiers and the United States Army was arranged for April 1867 at Pawnee Fork outside of Fort Larned, Kansas. Major General Winfield Hancock refused to talk with the Cheyenne until Roman Nose personally conferred with him. During the course of negotiations, Hancock moved his headquarters close to the Cheyenne lodges. This angered Roman Nose. Given the recent memory of the Sand Creek Massacre, the Cheyenne constantly feared for the safety of the women and children in camp. Roman Nose informed Hancock that the warriors were not afraid of his soldiers, and he bitingly remarked that Hancock's men looked "just like those who butchered the women and children" at Sand Creek.[41] Hancock in turn became alarmed when the women and children fled the village, claiming that this might indicate the Cheyenne were preparing for a fight. Hancock's response was to destroy the village. This only created further enmity between the Dog Soldiers and the United States.

On September 17, 1868, Roman Nose was killed while riding with Cheyenne Dog Soldiers, Sioux, and Arapaho warriors in an assault on a party of civilian scouts besieged on a small island in the Arickaree branch of the Republican River in eastern Colorado. The scouts, under the command of Col. George A. Forsyth, shot Roman Nose "in the small of the back as he passed" by their defense lines. His companions dragged him to safety, but he died within hours.[42] The Dog Soldiers lost a great hero and patriot for the cause of Cheyenne freedom.

Despite several military setbacks, the Dog Soldiers continued to clash openly with Cheyenne peace advocates. By 1869, the most influential proponent of compromise, a Southern Cheyenne chief named Little Robe, felt that the militant Dog Soldiers were detrimental to the welfare of the Cheyenne people. He banished them from his camp.[43] Little Robe was not a coward, but as a civil leader he felt it was his duty to pursue peace and preserve lives. He, like most peace chiefs of the Southern Cheyenne, was a realist and saw the futility in resisting the westward movement of settlers. He believed that the future of the Cheyenne rested in their ability to coexist peacefully in the same country with citizens of the United States. In 1874, during the Red River War, the Dog Soldiers quarreled with Little Robe once again. When the chief wanted to move his camp to the safe confines of the Darlington (Cheyenne-Arapaho) Indian Agency in [Oklahoma] Indian Territory, the Dog Soldiers voiced their opposition to this decision and shot Little Robe's horses.[44]

During the period 1865-1877, the Cheyenne were in continual conflict with the United States military. By the latter 1860s, the tide was slowly turning against the Cheyenne nation as the army gradually wore down Indian resistance. In early 1869, Cheyenne Dog Soldiers inflicted severe punishment on the Kansas frontier. This was partly in retaliation for the attack of George Custer and the Seventh Cavalry on Black Kettle's village on the Washita River in Indian Territory in November 1868, as noted above.[45] During this assault on this peaceful Cheyenne encampment, Black Kettle and his wife were killed. Over one hundred Cheyenne (mostly women and children) were killed or taken prisoner. Dog Soldiers also raided the frontier in response to an attack by Maj. Eugene A. Carr and seven troops of the Fifth Cavalry (led by William F. "Buffalo Bill" Cody) against a Dog Soldier hunting camp on the Republican River in May of 1869.[46]

Throughout the rest of May and June 1869, the Dog Soldiers led by Tall Bull and White Horse attacked white settlements in Jewell County, Kansas, and along the Solomon River in that state. They were aided by their Lakota allies, led by Whistler of the Oglalas and Two Strikes and his Brules. The raiders burned farmhouses, stole horses and mules, and attacked teamsters. They also derailed a train on the tracks of the Kansas Pacific Railroad.[47]

Units of the Seventh Cavalry under Custer were dispatched to Kansas to punish the Dogs but "caught only quick glimpses" of the Dog Soldiers, who moved too fast for the pursuing cavalrymen.[48] The Dog Men broke camp on the bison-rich Republican River and headed for the South Platte River, where they believed they would not be pursued. However, they postponed crossing to the greater safety of the far bank. On July 11, 1869, Carr's Fifth Cavalry, with three companies of Pawnee auxiliaries led by Capt. Luther North, caught up with Tall Bull's Dog Soldier band as they were camped at Summit Springs, Colorado. Tall Bull was killed during the battle, and Carr's command thereafter destroyed the village.[49]

Two Dog Soldiers in particular died in the courageous tradition of Cheyenne warriors. Little Hawk, a fifteen-year-old, had a chance to escape. Instead he held his ground and fought a rear guard action, which allowed many of the Cheyenne women and children to escape. It was said of him later that he gave "his life away for the People, as a brave man should" when the Pawnee scouts struck him down.[50] Another young Dog Soldier named Wolf With Plenty of Hair "staked himself out with a dog rope" in traditional fashion at the head of a ravine. The fighting around this man was very intense: "[N]o one had time to pull the picket pin for Wolf With Plenty of Hair." He was found dead in the place he had pinioned himself, having not retreated an inch.[51]

The Dog Soldiers lost over sixty men at Summit Springs , including a great leader. More seriously, they never regained their prominence as a separate political division of warriors.[52] Survivors trickled north to the camps of the Northern Cheyenne and Lakotas, while other Dog Soldiers joined the militant faction of the Southern Cheyenne located on the South Fork of the Canadian River in the Panhandle region of Texas. These Cheyenne in Texas would join forces with the Kiowas and Comanches in the Red River War of 1874.[53] In September of 1874, Colonel Nelson Miles and eight companies of the Sixth Cavalry, together with Colonel Ranald Mackenzie and seven troops of the Fourth Cavalry, invaded the Panhandle. The commanders launched a brutal winter campaign against the Southern Cheyenne and their Comanche and Kiowa allies. Pursued by troops and unable to establish a winter camp, these Indians and their ponies faced starvation and were unprotected from the freezing cold. By early 1875, the hostile elements of the Southern Cheyenne, including the remnants of the Dog Soldiers, were forced into submission and surrendered to Mackenzie. They agreed to live in exile and peace with other Southern Cheyenne and

Maj. Eugene Asa Carr

Generals in Blue

Arapahoes at the Darlington or Cheyenne-Arapaho Reservation Agency in Indian Territory.[54]

In the North, the annihilation of George Custer's command at the Little Bighorn in June of 1876 was the last major triumph of the Lakotas and Northern Cheyenne. In retaliation, the Northern Cheyenne were relentlessly pursued by eleven companies of cavalry under Mackenzie, along with his Pawnee and Shoshone scouts. The pursuit ended when they located and leveled the encampment of Dull Knife on November 26, 1876, in the Powder River country of Northern Wyoming on November 26, 1876.[55] The Northern Cheyenne, like their southern kin in Indian Territory, would be forced onto reservations.

Several Indian agents asked the military societies to help keep the peace among the Cheyenne. The Dog Soldiers were particularly sought out by reservation officials to carry out this duty.[56] But their obstinate nature and continued influence would pose a threat to government intentions. The Dog Soldiers reemerged during the reservation period of the 1880s as a force in opposition to the assimilation programs of agency officials. At Darlington Agency, Dog Soldiers at times harassed and humiliated those who tried to accept the government's policy of imposing the conquerors' social and economic systems.[57] Though the Dog Soldiers never approached the political and military power they once had, they remained revered by other Cheyenne. They are still held in respect today. Young Cheyenne are still recruited into this soldier clan. During the twentieth century, Dog Soldiers have served with the United States military in two world wars and in the conflicts in Korea, Vietnam, and the Persian Gulf region.

The rise of the Dog Soldiers demonstrated the dynamics of change among the Cheyenne and their ability to respond to a national crisis. The defeat at Summit Springs ended their prominence as a major force in opposition to United States expansion across the Great Plains. As Peter Powell succinctly stated, "With the defeat, the power of the Dog Men all but disappeared, blown away like wind blows the buffalo grass. The People," Powell continued, "never forgot their bravery."[58]

NOTES

1. George C. Brown of the *Cincinnati Commercial* in Stan Hoig, *The Battle of the Washita* (Lincoln: University of Nebraska Press, 1979), 33- 34.

2. Henry M. Stanley, "A British Journalist Reports the Medicine Lodge Peace Councils of 1867," *The Kansas Historical Quarterly* 23 (Autumn 1967): 305.

3. Billy Dixon, *Life of "Billy" Dixon*, ed. Olive K. Dixon (Dallas: P. L. Turner Company, 1927), 42.

4. Stanley, "British Journalist Reports," 310.

5. Hoig, *Battle of the Washita*, 34 and Donald J. Berthrong, *The Southern Cheyenne* (Norman: University of Oklahoma Press, 1963), 294-299.

6. K. N. Llewellyn and E. Adamson Hoebel, *The Cheyenne Way: Conflict and Case Law in Primitive Jurisprudence* (Norman: University of Oklahoma Press, 1967), 104.

7. John Stands In Timber and Margot Liberty, with the assistance of Robert M. Utley, *Cheyenne Memories* (New Haven: Yale University Press, 1967), 193.

8. Ibid., 34-35. For information on Cheyenne tribal structure see John H. Moore, *The Cheyenne Nation* (Lincoln: University of Nebraska Press, 1987); 232-249. Moore gave a detailed explanation of the Cheyenne origin as large groups of Algonquin-speaking people. In earlier times they included the *Tsistsistas, Heviksnipahis, Hevhaitaneo, Ovimana* and *Hisiometaneo*. Later, during the early 1800s, the body known as the Cheyenne proper, came together with linguistically related people in the Black Hills who spoke a similar language. These were the *Sutaio, Omisis* and the *Masikota* and *Watapio*. The later two were considered to be groups of mixed Sioux blood. According to Moore, these bands were kinship units and comprised the Cheyenne nation. Bands were flexible and free to move about to new locations. They could camp with other groups whenever they choose. In *The Fighting Cheyenne*, Grinnell offered a less complicated explanation. He contended that the Cheyenne were a merger of the *Tsistsistas* and *Sutaio*. But he also maintained that as late as the 1830s bands of *Sutaio* people retained their identity as a group separate from the Cheyenne. See George Bird Grinnell, *The Fighting Cheyenne* (1915; reprint, Norman: University of Oklahoma Press, 1985), 3-4. E. Adamson Hoebel defined Tsistsistas as meaning "The People" or "Human Beings." Both terms according to Hoebel symbolized Plains Indian "elemental ethnocentrism." See E. Adamson Hoebel, *The Cheyenne: Indians Of The Great Plains*, (1960; reprint, Chicago: Holt, Rinehart and Winston, Inc., 1978), 4-5.

9. George Bent in George E. Hyde, *Life of George Bent, Written From His Letters*, ed. Savoie Lottinville (Norman: University of Oklahoma Press, 1987), 337. Grinnell listed a seventh, the Chief Soldiers, but Thomas Mails maintains that the group called the Chief Soldiers were the same group as the Council of Forty-four and that they were certainly not a military society. See Thomas E. Mails, *Plains Indians: Dog Soldiers, Bear Men and Buffalo Women* (New York: Bonanza Books, 1985), 320-321.

10. Hyde, *Life of George Bent*, 337.

11. Mails, *Dog Soldiers, Bear Men*, 330.

12. Mails, *Dog Soldiers, Bear Men*, 330; See George Bird Grinnell, *Cheyenne Indians: Their History and Ways of Life*, vol. 2, (1923; reprint, New York: Cooper Square Publishers, Inc. 1962), 67-69. Grinnell stated that Cheyenne called this dog rope *Hotamtsit*.

13. Anthony McGinnis, *Counting Coup and Cutting Horses: Intertribal Warfare on The Northern Plains, 1738-1889* (Evergreen, Colorado: Cordillera Press, Inc., 1990), 93.

14. Wooden Leg in *Wooden Leg: A Warrior Who Fought Custer*, edited by Thomas Marquis (1931; reprint, Lincoln: University of Nebraska Press, 1988), 120-121.

15. Richard Irving Dodge, *The Plains of The Great West and Their Inhabitants* (1885; reprint, New York: Archer House, Inc., 1959), 267.

16. Llewellyn and Hoebel, *Cheyenne Way*, 114-115.

17. Dodge, *Plains of The Great West*, 277.

18. George Bent in Hyde, *Life of George Bent*, 74. In Grinnell's version, Porcupine Bear and his men brought kegs of whiskey with them as presents for the chiefs of the camps. See George B. Grinnell, *The Fighting Cheyenne* (1915; reprint, Norman: University of Oklahoma Press, 1985), 49.

19. Grinnell, *Fighting Cheyenne*, 49.

20. George Bent in Hyde, *Life of George Bent*, 74-75.

21. Stan Hoig, *The Peace Chiefs of the Cheyenne* (Norman: University of Oklahoma Press, 1980), 49.

22. Llewellyn and Hoebel, *Cheyenne Way*, 100. Also see Grinnell, *Cheyenne Indians*, 63.

23. Karen D. Petersen, "Cheyenne Soldier Societies," *Plains Anthropologist* (Aug. 1964), 154-155. While Petersen has recognized the Dog Soldiers as a separate division of the Cheyenne, free of the control of civil chiefs, she has also pointed out their continued importance as part of the Cheyenne nation. They unified and stabilized the Cheyenne people in these times of uncertainty. In her words, "as the emigrants drove a wedge between the Southern Cheyenne and the Northern, the Dog Soldiers exercised a magnetic force pulling the tribe together" (55).

24. Thomas Fitzpatrick in John J. Killoren, *Come, Blackrobe* (Norman: University of Oklahoma Press, 1994), 193.

25. William Bent in Killoren, *Come, Blackrobe*, 209.

26. John H. Moore, *The Cheyenne Nation* (Lincoln: University of Nebraska Press, 1987), 196.

27. Moore, *The Cheyenne Nation*, 198. Moore maintained that the Masikota band of Cheyenne were absorbed into the Dog Soldiers in the late 1840s. They were weakened by the cholera epidemic of 1849 and camped with the Dog Soldiers for military protection. The Masikota were believed by Moore to be a people with mixed Sioux blood. Eventually they lost their identity as Masikota and referred to themselves as "Flint Men," 238-239.

28. Petersen, "Cheyenne Soldier Societies," 195.

29. E. Adamson Hoebel, "On Cheyenne Socio-Political Organization," *Plains Anthropologist* (May 1980): 164.

30. Elbridge Gerry in Berthrong, *The Southern Cheyenne*, 204.

31. Grinnell, *Fighting Cheyenne*, 133-134; Llewellyn and Hoebel, *Cheyenne Way*, 105. The Dog Soldiers felt that during the negotiation of the Treaty of Fort Wise in 1861 the chiefs had been bribed into signing away part of the Republican and Smoky Hill

territory. They feared that Bull Bear would be inclined to agree with the peace chiefs and cede additional hunting ground.

32. George E. Fay, ed., *Military Engagements Between United States Troops And Plains Indians: Documentary Inquiry By The U.S. Congress*, Part Ib 1854-1867 (Greeley, Colorado: Museum of Anthropology, University of Northern Colorado, 1972), 117, 124. These documents include testimony delivered by Governor Evans on March 15, 1865, regarding the slaughter of over 130 Cheyenne and Arapahoes at Sand Creek. See also Stan Hoig, *The Sand Creek Massacre* (Norman: University of Oklahoma Press, 1961).

33. Ben Clark in Petersen, "Cheyenne Soldier Societies," 154.

34. George Bent in Moore, *Cheyenne Nation*, 198.

35. Moore, *Cheyenne Nation*, 196-197,

36. Ibid., 196.

37. Ibid., 197.

38. Hoig, *Peace Chiefs of the Cheyenne*, 96.

39. George Bent in Orvel A. Criqui, "A Northern Cheyenne Called Roman Nose," *Kansas History*, 8 (Autumn 1985): 180.

40. Dee Brown, *Bury My Heart At Wounded Knee* (New York: Henry Holt and Company, 1991), 94-96.

41. Roman Nose to Maj. Gen. Winfield Hancock in Ibid.,148.

42. George Bent in Criqui, "A Northern Cheyenne Called Roman Nose," 177-178. This battle was known by the whites as the Beecher Island Fight while Cheyenne called it the "Fight When Roman Nose Was Killed." See Brown, *Bury My Heart At Wounded Knee*, 166. According to George Bent, Roman Nose could not eat food that had been touched by metal for his "medicine spirit" told him that metal attracted bullets. Earlier that day he unknowingly had eaten fry bread that a Sioux woman had served with an iron fork. When he found this out, he knew that his medicine (spiritual guidance and empowerment) would fail him. However, the Cheyenne leaders Bull Bear and White Horse "begged him to lead a charge" and drive the scouts from their position. Roman Nose "could not resist the temptation and went to his death." See George Bent in Hyde, *Life of George Bent*, 95-100.

43. James L. Haley, *The Buffalo War: The History of The Red River Indian Uprising of 1874* (Norman: University of Oklahoma Press, 1985), 38.

44. Ibid., 56-57; Hoig, *Peace Chiefs of the Cheyenne*, 148-150. Little Robe was at one time a Dog Soldier leader of prominence. His father, who was one of the forty-four chiefs, was killed at Sand Creek in 1864. Little Robe left the Dog Soldiers to take his father's place in this council. He became despised by the Dogs because of his pro-peace policy. See Peter Powell, *People of the Sacred Mountain: A History of the Northern Cheyenne Chiefs and Warrior Societies, 1830-1879* , vol. II (San Francisco: Harper & Row, Publishers, 1981), 839.

45. See Hoig, *Battle of the Washita* for a full account of this Cheyenne tragedy.

46. Powell, *People of the Sacred Mountain*, 724.

47. Ibid., 725.

48. Ibid., 725-726. Custer referred to the Cheyenne as Kite Indians, for they quickly moved camp, and from a distance they resembled a flying kite in the wind.

49. Grinnell, *Fighting Cheyenne*, 310-318; Hyde, *Life of George Bent*, 330-335; Moore, *Cheyenne Nation*,199; Powell, *People of the Sacred Mountain*, 722-735; and Jean Afton and others, eds., *Cheyenne Dog Soldiers: A Ledgerbook History of Coups and Combat* (Niwot, Colorado: University Press of Colorado, 1997), xix, 284, and 320. According to George Bent, William Cody claimed to have killed Tall Bull.

50. Powell, *People of the Sacred Mountain*, 735.

51. George Bent in Hyde, *Life of George Bent*, 334.

52. Powell, *People of the Sacred Mountain*, 735.

53. Moore, *Cheyenne Nation*, 101-102 and Hyde, *Life of George Bent*, 334-335.

54. Haley, *Buffalo War*, 193,195, 208-209.

55. Grinnell, *Fighting Cheyenne*, 359-361.

56. Moore, *Cheyenne Nation* , 132.

57. For more information on reservation-era Dog Soldiers, see Donald J. Berthrong, *The Cheyenne and Arapaho Ordeal: Reservation and Agency Life in The Indian Territory, 1875-1907* (Norman: University of Oklahoma Press, 1976) and Charles C. Bush, "The Cheyenne-Arapaho Disturbances of 1884-1885," 7, Western History Collections, Charles C. Bush Collection: Box 3, Folder 2, The University of Oklahoma Libraries, Norman, Oklahoma.

58. Powell, *People of the Sacred Mountain*, 735.

FORSYTH'S SCOUTS

at the Battle of Beecher Island

Kerry R. Oman

Of men who have a sense of honor, more come through alive than are slain, but from those who flee comes neither glory nor any help.

Homer, *The Iliad*

T he tale of the Battle of Beecher Island may seem an American *Iliad*, lacking only a Homer to complete the transformation of history into poetry. For nine long days, September 17 to 25, 1868, fifty frontier scouts on a small island in the Arickaree Fork of the Republican River fought for their lives against hundreds of Cheyenne, Sioux, and Arapaho Indians. Like the *Iliad's* Greeks during an assault on the beach near ancient Troy, the handful of recruits held on to a vital stretch of sand against anywhere from ten to one to twenty to one odds. Like the ancient epic's Trojans, the Indian forces lost their invincible champion as the result of a prophecy of doom. Unlike Homer's heroes, however, it was quick thinking, superior weapons, and a a fortunate location that made the difference between life and death for Major George A. Forsyth's men.

The Plains Indian War of 1867-1869 was a resumption of hostilities between two very different cultures fighting for the possession of territory each claimed. During the latter part of the American Civil War (1861-1865), traffic to Rocky Mountain goldfields, opportunistic raids by young warriors, and misdirected attacks by Colorado state volunteers had incited mistrust and revenge across the central Great Plains. The period from 1866 to early 1867 saw a lessening of the violence with the negotiation of the ambiguous Treaty of the Little Arkansas River and the Treaty of Medicine Lodge Creek [both in Kansas].

But tensions soon heightened again. Settlement and railway construction were rapidly advancing west from Kansas. Prospector and freight traffic to Colorado across Southern Cheyenne (*Tsistsistas*) and Southern Arapaho (*Inunaina*) territory increased. A punitive expedition under Gen. Winfield Scott Hancock stirred hostilities even as the powerful Cheyenne warrior societies became increasingly militant. In 1868, Cheyenne and Arapaho raiding parties began to strike settlements in the Smoky Hill, Saline and Solomon River valleys. By the summer of 1868, the outcry from affected Nebraska, Kansas, and Colorado settlers led Gen. Phillip Sheridan to pledge that he would do all he could to "clean up the Indians."[1]

Sheridan planned to utilize Plains frontiersmen as scouts in an attempt to keep a closer watch on the "hostile" Indians. Meanwhile, Maj. George A. "Sandy" Forsyth, who had ridden with Sheridan at the Battle of Winchester, Virginia, during the Civil War, went to the general on August 24, 1866, to plead that Sheridan transfer him from staff duties to field command in the upcoming campaign. Forsyth requested that Sheridan "in case opportunity offered, would kindly consider [his] request for the first field vacancy."[2] Approximately an hour later, Forsyth was ordered to immediately employ fifty "first-class hardy frontiersmen" to be used as "scouts against the hostile Indians." These recruits were to be under Forsth's command with 1st Lt. Frederick H. Beecher serving as his subordinate. The details of how these scouts were to be employed were to be worked out between Forsyth and his men, allowing Forsyth the liberty to do whatever was needed to guarantee their faithful service.[3]

Forsyth began to enlist scouts at Fort Harker, Kansas, which was not a difficult task as most of the frontiersman had felt the effects of the Indian raiding parties or knew someone who had. John Hurst, who enlisted at Fort Harker, recalled that he was prompted to join the unit by "love of adventure," which he claimed was "inherent in all American frontiersmen."[4] Forsyth was able to recruit thirty men at Fort Harker and twenty more men at Fort Hays, approximately sixty miles to the west. Many of these men already had some military experience from the Civil War. Their compensation for serving as scouts was to be $50 a month for those who had to draw government horses and $75 a month for those who used their own stock.[5]

Maj. George A. "Sandy" Forsyth

Kansas State Historical Society, Topeka, Kansas

By the end of August, the men were ready to take the field. Since they were designed to serve as a fast moving mobile unit, their equipment was light. Each man was issued a blanket, saddle and bridle, a lariat, picket pin, canteen, haversack, butcher knife, tin plate, and tin cup. However, the most important item each man received was a Spencer repeating rifle. These relatively new weapons held seven bullets—six in the magazine and one in the chamber—and every man carried 140 rounds of ammunition. Along with the rifles, all of the scouts carried a Colt revolver pistol and thirty rounds of ammunition. In addition, each scout carried with him seven days of cooked rations in his haversack. Only four pack mules accompanied the men. One was loaded down with 4,000 extra rounds of ammunition; another packed medical equipment, and the remaining two carried other necessary supplies.[6]

Early in the morning on August 29, Forsyth was ordered by General Sheridan to "move across the head-waters of [the] Solomon [River] to Beaver Creek, thence down that creek to Fort Wallace." Upon their arrival at that post, Forsyth was to report to Sheridan by telegraph.[7] Around 2:00 in the afternoon, Forsyth's troops set out from Fort Hayes on the assigned and circuitous route to Fort Wallace. Lieutenant Frederick Beecher acted as their guide. From Fort Hayes, the party crossed over the Saline River and the South Fork of the Solomon, and then hit Beaver Creek where Short Nose Creek empties into it. They followed Beaver Creek to its source, then crossed over to the Little Beaver.[8]

Several of the newly recruited scouts were not accustomed to such hard riding, and constant rubbing of the saddle quickly took effect. "I shall never forget this first day's ride!" recalled Sigmund Schlesinger:

> I was not used to the saddle, and my equipment, consisting of carbine, revolvers, saddlebags, roll of blankets, etc., was always where it should not have been. I could not adjust all this paraphernalia so that I could be comfortable. My horse would not stay with the column, but forged ahead, being a fast walker, causing me to be ordered back into line several times. My bridle arm became stiff and lame in the effort to obey; every bone in my body began to ache; the ride and the day seemed never to end, and with every mile's travel my misery was bordering on torture. I was chafed by the saddle, and some parts became swollen to twice the normal size; my gun would never stay in place; and to add to my troubles, my clothes became wet from a drizzling rain, making the skin tender where belts attempted to hold the equipment in place.

However, Schlesinger added, "[I]t did not take many days for everybody, myself included, to become hardened and fit to meet emergencies incidental to life on the prairie."[9]

Forsyth's scouts marched into Fort Wallace on September 5, having been out a week without seeing any Cheyenne or Arapaho. However, as the scouts

Sigmund Schlesinger

Kansas State Historical Society, Topeka, Kansas

were approaching Fort Wallace, they were ordered to charge up a hill that was thought to be occupied by Indians. Instead, the "Indians" turned out to be some haymakers returning from Fort Wallace who had hidden themselves in the belief that Forsyth's men were Indians. One scout was thrown from his horse in the charge and was injured so badly that he had to receive medical attention at the fort.[10]

While the scouts were resting at Fort Wallace, word was received that a raiding party had attacked some traders near Sheridan, Kansas. Two teamsters had been killed and some of their stock captured. Sheridan, then the western terminus of the Kansas Pacific Railroad, was only thirteen miles east of the fort. Immediately Forsyth and his scouts set out, carrying only six days of rations. When they arrived at the scene of the raid, Forsyth was able to conclude that the attack had been made by twenty to twenty-five warriors (not three hundred, as he had been told at Fort Wallace). After a close examination of the surrounding area, the scouts located the escape trail of the raiding party and at once set out in pursuit.[11] However, the traces soon began to thin out and before long disappeared altogether. Knowing they were being followed, the Indians had scattered and taken to terrain where the ground was hard and would leave few tracks. After some discussion, the troops continued on toward the Republican River, determined to find and attack the hostile Indians.[12]

Upon reaching the Republican, the scouts found a small shelter which some Indians had recently formed by bending over saplings and tying the trees together. With a little more effort, a trail was spotted and the men set off upon it. This time the trail became more distinct, and soon they noticed the marks made by lodge poles that had been tied together to form the travoises dragged behing Indian ponies. The marks were a sure sign that the scouts were close behind a moving village of Indians and not just a war party. As the trail grew, some of the men worried that it was dangerous for their small party of scouts to follow so closely behind such a large trail. They feared that they would soon overtake the Indians and be met with overwhelming numbers.

Forsyth's answer to the apprehension was quick and to the point. He told the men "that they were assuming no risk that [he] was not taking [himself]."[13] And then he challenged them: "Well! Did you men not enlist to fight Indians?"[14] This ended the discussion, but did not convince everyone of the wisdom of close pursuit. The scouts camped early on the night of September 16 in a beautiful valley rich in grass, where their tired horses grazed freely and regained some strength. Their camp was on the north side of the Arickaree Fork of the Republican River, overlooking a large island in the largely dry riverbed.[15]

Meanwhile, the Indians had reached their main village, unaware that the scouts were following them. This village consisted of two large bands of Brule Lakota Sioux, under Pawnee Killer and one group of [primarily Northern] Cheyenne, along with a few Northern Arapaho. Apart from the famed warrior Roman Nose, the Cheyenne were mainly members of the Dog Soldier warrior society. This elite group included other great fighting men such as Tall Bull (Hotoakhihpois) and White Horse.[16] Forsyth's men were spotted by a Lakota Sioux war party returning from a raid on the South Platte River. The Indians watched the scouts until late in the day and then brought the news to their village. As criers spread the news, the warriors began preparing for battle. In the midst of this, two Cheyenne warriors who had been out hunting came in and reported seeing the soldiers only twelve miles up the Republican River. Upon this news, an admonition was sent through all the villages saying that all the men must wait and proceed together as one force.[17]

At this time one of the greatest and most respected warriors of the Northern Cheyenne was Roman Nose (Woqini). In an 1866 council held at Fort Ellsworth, Kansas, General Rodenbough wrote this colorful description of the famed warrior:

> Roman Nose moved in a solemn and majestic manner to the center of the chamber. He was one of the finest specimens of the untamed savage. It would be difficult to exaggerate in describing his superb physique. A veritable man of war, the shock of battle and scenes of carnage and cruelty were as the breath of his nostrils; about thirty years of age, standing six feet three inches high, he towered, giant-like, above his companions. A grand head, with strongly marked features, lighted by a pair of fierce black eyes; a large mouth with thin lips, through which gleamed rows of strong white teeth; a Roman nose, with delicate nostrils like those of a thoroughbred horse, first attracted attention, while a broad chest, with symmetrical limbs, on which the muscles under the bronze of his skin stood out like twisted wire, were some of the points of this splendid animal. Clad in buckskin leggings and moccasins, elaborately embroidered with beads and feathers, with a single eagle feather in his scalp-lock, and that rarest of robes, a white buffalo, beautifully tanned and as soft as cashmere, thrown over his naked shoulders, he stood forth, the war-chief of the Cheyennes.[18]

Sioux and Cheyenne warriors. From left to right: Spotted Tail
(Brule Sioux), Roman Nose (Cheyenne, seated), and
Old Man Afraid of His Horse (Dakota Sioux).

Western History Collections, University of Oklahoma Libraries

Roman Nose was never a chief, but was a tremendous warrior and a natural
leader in war. He was a member of the Crooked Lance Society, but liked the
wild Dog Soldiers and lived and fought with them. In battle, Roman Nose wore
a famous war bonnet, the only one of its kind, made for him by White Buffalo

Bull. Instead of having two buffalo horns attached to the head-band, it had only one. (After fasting for four days on an island in a Montana lake, as a boy, Roman Nose had seen in his visions a serpent with a single horn in its head. Believing this to be a sign, he had a single horn placed on the war bonnet.) The bonnet also had a very long tail lined with eagle feathers, which nearly touched the ground.[19]

The Plains Indian act of going into battle traditionally required much ceremony. Roman Nose had a particularly strict set of rules and riturals concerning both the war bonnet and the sacred "medicine" paint he put on before battle. These rules had to be followed closely for the medicine (spiritual protection and power) to work. One such rule was that Roman Nose could never eat anything that had been touched by metal. The warrior had been told that if he ever violated this prohibition he would be killed in his next battle. Roman Nose was always very careful in observing the rules and felt protected because of it. With his great medicine safeguarding him, Roman Nose was consistently in the front of his battles and rarely had a horse shot from under him.[20]

Prior to the discovery of Forsyth's scouts, a feast was given by the Lakotas at which Roman Nose was an invited guest. At the feast he began talking with the chiefs and forgot to tell the Lakota women not to use metal in preparing his food. It wasn't until the meal was over that Roman Nose found out the woman who prepared his meal had taken his bread from the frying pan with an iron fork. His medicine had been violated. Tall Bull, another superior war leader, advised Roman Nose to immediately go through the long purification ceremony required to bring back his medicine. However, just as this was happening word came through camp that Forsyth's men were moving, and Roman Nose had no time to go through the ceremony.[21]

As the warriors rushed to get their best war horses, Roman Nose sent word to the Cheyenne to go on without him. He knew his protection was gone, and he would come when he was ready to die. Finally, when prepared, the Cheyenne, Arapaho, and Lakota warriors set off together in one group carrying shields, lances, bows, and the few muzzle-loading guns they possessed. All of the warriors had on their war regalia, including their paint and talismans. They rode hard until nightfall, but could not find Forsyth's scouts, who were now twenty miles away. Orders were given to rest where they were; when the morning star came up, they would start out again.[22]

At this point several young warriors seized the opportunity to make a name for themselves by being the first to contact the enemy. They slipped out to find the army scouts. Two Cheyenne, Starving Elk and Little Hawk, leading six Lakotas, scouted around in the darkness looking for light from the scouts' fires. The warriors rode from hill to hill, stopping to listen for any sounds from their enemy's encampment. This process was repeated all through the night as the warriors searched for several miles in the darkness. It was just before daylight when a glimpse of Forsyth's campfires was finally spotted. Riding quietly toward the camp, the young warriors halted just close enough to see the scouts' horses and mules. They were an enticing prize. With a rush, the young warriors charged through the picketed horses, all the while yelling and waving robes and blankets in an effort to stampede the animals. However, only seven animals broke loose from their picket pins (stakes for tethers) and were stampeded by this surprise charge.[23]

Earlier that evening the party of scouts, nervous and wary but still unaware of how close they were to the Indians' bivouac, had settled down to sleep by the nearly dry Arickaree Fork of the Republican River. John Hurst and Thomas Murphy were the first to carry out guard duty. Hurst recalled the night: "We cooked some beans for the men who were to relieve us, and had a square meal ourselves—our last, by the way, for nine long, weary days."[24] After their watch was finished, Hurst and Murphy were relieved by two other men, and were soon fast asleep. The two used their saddles for pillows and kept their guns at their side.[25]

Forsyth's cry of "Indians! Turn out! Indians!" along with the crack of rifle shots immediately brought the sleeping camp awake.[26] As the scouts tried to determine what was happening, Starving Elk and his small party yelled and chased the seven horses away. This brought the scouts running to the other frightened animals. Following Forsyth's orders, they quickly saddled up and made ready to ride. As they awaited the next order, young Louis Farley saw a mounted warrior coming down off a hill. If someone would go with him, he shouted, he would try to get a shot at the Indian. Eli Zigler volunteered to accompany Farley. As the two rode over the hill, the warrior was still in sight but remained out of range. Farley and Zigler decided to continue on over the next hill, which overlooked the stream. Upon reaching the crest of the second rise, the scouts saw the main party of Indians waiting below. As they stood in amazement at the tremendous numbers of warriors [500-600 by several estimates], Zigler recalled. "All of a sudden the Indians mounted up and started down the river and others came over the bluff." As the warriors mounted their ponies, "it looked as though the whole bottom [riverbed] rose up."[27] The two hurried back and warned the other scouts, shouting at them to look up the creek. There "Indians by the hundreds were everywhere in full view. They seemed to spring from the very earth," John Hurst later remembered, concluding that "it was the most thrilling sight" he had ever seen.[28]

The scouts's immediate challenge was to find a place where they could defend themselves against the huge war party. Within the Arickaree Fork lay a sandy island nearly 150 feet long and 75 feet wide. It rose several feet above the bed of shallow stream and was covered in grass nearly four feet high, along with with bushy willows, alders, and one cottonwood tree. Jack Stillwell suggested that they all go to the island for shelter rather than try to run. This seemed the best choice, and Forsyth gave the order for the men to make their way to the island. As the scouts reached it, they tied their animals to the trees and bushes and scattered to seek shelter in the tall grass. Before all the man had made their way across the almost dry riverbed, the warriors came rushing toward them. It seemed that the fight would not last more than a few moments. The island, however, provided a haven that would make the difference between life and death.[29]

Though terrifying, the onset of the charge was not without a moment of humor. As the Indians were thundering toward the scouts, Marin Burke discovered that he would not make it to the island before the Indians reached him. He lay in the cover of some brush by the stream and fought as best he could while the warriors raced all around him. Then he saw an Indian about 200 yards away, crawling towards the scouts' island position. Wanting to make sure he could hit the Indian, Burke decided to creep up a small elevation to get a better shot. As he made his way up to the top of the rise, he lifted himself on his hands and knees to take a look. To his surprise, the warrior on the other side was in the act of doing the very same thing. Both men were shocked by the sight of each other. "Instead of shooting the Indian [Burke] merely poked his gun at him and cried 'BOO,' then took to his heels as fast as he could and ran to the island where the rest of the men were." Burke did not hear any shots fired after him, although he dared not look back. He eventually reasoned that the Indian had raced away as he had.[30]

On the island, the scouts found themselves in a desperate situation. All about them rode mounted warriors. In response, the scouts positioned themselves throughout the small piece of acreage and began throwing up breastworks and digging rifle pits as best they could. Their horses and mules were easy targets for the Indians' rapid fire, and soon most of them were killed.

Amid the chaos of the situation, Forsyth stood giving orders to his men, ignoring their constant pleas for him to take cover. Just as Forsyth recognized the wisdom of their concern, a bullet smashed into his upper right thigh and lodged itself next to his leg bone. "Is there anyone here who can pray?" he asked. "We are beyond human help and if God doesn't help there is no hope for us?"[31]

The only physician in the group, Dr. J. H. Moores, was close by. He suggested that the scouts enlarge his pit so that he could attend to the major. As

Dr. J. H. Moores

Forsyth knelt next to the doctor, another bullet crushed into his lower left leg. This time the lead slug shattered the bone between the knee and the ankle. Just moments later, a bullet struck Moores in the head. The unfortunate doctor lingered in agony for three days before expiring. The carnage was only beginning. A bullet struck Lieutenant Beecher in his side, a painful wound that proved fatal. By now the last of the horses had also been felled. As bullets zipped through the air and men on both sides were struck down, several scouts

Lt. Frederick Beecher

Kansas State Historical Society, Topeka, Kansas

heard someone in the Indian ranks cry out in good English, "There goes the last damned horse, anyhow!"[32]

With this, the warriors assembled to make the first concerted charge of the day. Since Roman Nose was still back at the village, Bad Heart, a great shaman who wore a panther skin over his shoulder, led the assault.[33] The Indians galloped towards the island in a rush, shooting and shouting at the top of their lungs. Some Indians were blowing bird-bone whistles, the use of which was thought to protect a warrior from bullets during combat. Many of the Lakotas wore magnificent eagle-feathered war bonnets, while the Cheyenne Dog Soldiers were capped by their own distinctive crow-feathered bonnets. As the warriors surged forward, the scouts' advantage in weaponry was quickly obvious as they poured bullets into the Indian ranks. Used to the old muzzle loading guns, the warriors did not understand how the scouts were able to reload so quickly. Soon the constant fire was enough to scatter the charge, and the warriors split to each side of the scouts' position. Only one man, Bad Heart, raced directly at the low island. He rode right over it and the men upon it amid a hail of bullets from the Spencer repeaters. He then turned and returned over the island in defiance of everything Forsyth's men could fire at him. Remarkably, Bad Heart and his pony concluded the exploit without a scratch.[34]

While the rest of the scouts were scattered upon the island, Jack Stillwell and another man had positioned themselves in tall grass on the river bank, just off the lower end of the island. The Indians circled the recruits, unaware of the pair's position. A warrior named Weasel Bear unknowingly charged straight at the two hidden scouts. Just before he was on top of them, Stillwell and his partner shot him, and Weasel Bear fell dead from his pony. As often happened, many of the bravest acts of courage performed by the Indians in a battle occurred while trying to rescue the body of a dead or wounded warrior. This engagement was no exception. White Thunder, the nephew of Weasel Bear, courageously tried to recover his uncle's body, only to be shot down by the same two men who had killed his relative.[35]

The warriors reformed and made a second charge. This time it was easily stopped by the rapid fire of the Spencers before they reached the point of the island. After this second mounted attempt to overrun the island, one of the chiefs called out to the warriors to instead go forward on foot. Good Bear, Prairie Bear, and Little Man were among several men who ran toward the stream bank and began digging holes from which to strike the scouts. Their position lacked good cover, however, and as Prairie Bear and Little Man raised

Jack Stillwell, Arikaree scout

Kansas State Historical Society, Topeka, Kansas

themselves to fire, both were shot in the head and killed. Frightened, Good Bear leapt up and sprinted for safety, dodging bullets as he sought a safe haven. After this incident, the warriors finally discovered the position of the two scouts shooting from the bank.[36]

During the early hours of the battle, Forsyth's command had suffered tremendously from the Indian fire. Several of the men had gathered together and excavated holes in the sand for protection. Once the horses were dead, John Hurst, W. M. McCall, and G. W. Culver began to improve their position by digging in behind the carcasses. Still, in order to shoot, they had to rise up and expose themselves to enemy fire. Almost immediately a bullet struck McCall in the neck before glancing off and hitting Culver in the head, instantly killing him. During a brief lull, Hurst called over to his comrades to see how they fared, only to learn from the wounded McCall that Culver was dead. Hurst had taken off his cartridge belt and had unknowingly buried it in the sand while digging his pit. Culver's death provided the embattled scout with an opportunity to replenish his ammunition. "If Culver is dead," he shouted to McCall, "throw me his cartridge box." It was no time to worry about the propriety of taking objects from the dead.[37]

Another scout, Frank Harrington, staggered over to the now blood soaked pits. He had been struck in the head by an arrow, and the point was still lodged in his skull. Several men attempted to extract it, but were unsuccessful. Miraculously, an Indian bullet struck Harrington in the skull and knocked out the arrow. Relieved, Harrington took cover and continued to defend the island as best he could.[38]

After the Indians dismounted and began to approach the island on foot, runners were sent to the village to call up Roman Nose. Although his medicine was now powerless, Roman Nose headed straight for the battlefield. However, he arrived late in the day after the fighting had abated. Roman Nose stopped at the top of a point overlooking the river and was met by Tall Bull and White Horse. They knew that his supernatural protection was gone, and they were concerned for his welfare. However, the arrival of Roman Nose excited the warriors, and they now waited to see what he would do. An elder, White Contrary, rode up to Roman Nose and reproached him for not coming to the battleground sooner. Roman Nose defended the delay by telling White Contrary how he had lost his medicine from eating food lifted with an iron utensil. He then bravely stated, "I know that I shall be killed today." At this point one of the chiefs asked him to lead the next charge. Roman Nose accepted the honor and challenge without hesitation.[39]

Roman Nose rode aside to paint himself for battle and put on the war bonnet that had been part of his spiritual protection. Mounting his war pony, he led what would be the fifth and final charge of the day. Riding at full speed, he

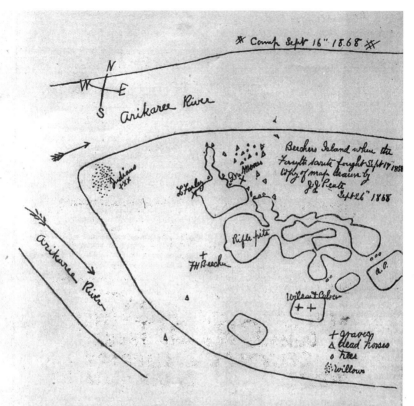

MAP OF BEECHER ISLAND.

The above map is reproduced from a copy drawn by J. J. Peate, of the Relief Expedition, at the time Forsyth and his scouts were rescued by Col. Carpenter's command.

The Island appears today as it did then excepting that the south channel of the river is closed and the trees and improvements, including the monument, appear as the Association has placed them.

This map was drawn by J. J. Peale, a member of the Relief Expedition, shortly after Forsyth's men were rescued.

unknowingly headed directly toward the spot where Stillwell and his companion were still hidden in the tall grass. The loud pounding and splashing of the charge was answered with a torrent of fire from the island, first and foremost by the two hidden scouts. A bullet penetrated the great warrior's body just above the hips. Barely able to stay on his pony, Roman Nose rode back to the Indian lines, where he dismounted and lay on the ground. Bull Bear and White Horse immediately rode up and found their great war leader dying. Some women came over and took the wounded man back to camp. Roman Nose would die before seeing the next sunrise.[40]

During the day, a small party led by Cloud Chief risked their lives to remove the bodies of White Thunder and Weasel Bear. Recovering the fallen was a very dangerous but important task to most Plains warriors. As nightfall approached, they crept through the tall grass along the stream banks, even though the scouts shot whenever they saw the grass quiver. The warriors crawled cautiously until they reached the two bodies. It was an expensive bit of bravado. While edging forward, every member of the group except Two Crows was struck, although most of the injuries were flesh wounds. Cloud Chief wrapped a rope around White Thunder's foot and dragged him away. When they found Weasel Bear, they discovered he was actually still alive but unable to move his legs. The lariat Cloud Chief was carrying was used to remove him to safety.[41]

None of Forsyth's men had ever waited so anxiously for nightfall as they did that first day of the battle. Thankfully, the Indians departed for the night, and it also began to rain. The water provided relief after the blistering daytime heat. The welcomed darkness helped hide the scouts and gave them a chance to rest, regroup, and strengthen their crude entrenchments. The scouts had managed to save 4,000 rounds of ammunition from the pack mule as they were crossing over to the island, and set about retrieving cartridges from their individual saddlebags. The scouts also found a few shovels and, following Forsyth's orders, connected all of the rifle pits into a continous line. Earlier in the day, Martin Burke had been digging one such hole and happened to dig deep enough to reach water below the surface. This excavation was later enlarged to the point that all were able to drink freely from it.[42]

With the setting sun, Forsyth's men were finally able to gather and care for the wounded. A large central pit was dug in which they could protect the injured from the attacks that morning would surely bring. Those scouts who were still able helped gather the saddles and blankets off the dead horses and made the best beds that they could for the injured. A list of the wounded was then brought to Forsyth: five men were dead or dying, and nearly twenty others were wounded to some degree.[43]

Unfortunately, the column's medical supplies had been left behind in the rush to the island and had fallen into the hands of the Indians. Also, when the scouts went into camp that night (16th), they were nearly out of supplies. Hence, after the first day of battle, there was nothing left to eat, and the men were forced to cut steaks off the dead horses and mules. In an attempt to make this limited and perishable food supply last longer, they hung the meat on the surrounding trees and bushes to dry. Several men declared they would rather starve than eat horse meat, but they eventually gave in and devoured the flesh. That night the men dined on a supper of raw horse, afraid that if they built a fire the warriors would be able to pick them off.[44]

With so many men wounded and uable to move, they would have to remain on the island until help arrived. In talking with the group's chief guide, scout Sharp Grover, Major Forsyth inquired what the chances would be of two men reaching Fort Wallace for help. Grover magnified the dangers and said that any attempt would be futile since the warriors would surely have every escape route cut off. However, Jack Stillwell spoke up. "He didn't care how alert the Indians might be—if someone was willing to accompany him he would go." An older scout named Pierre Trudeau also volunteered. Forsyth consented, and the pair of brave men set out with a dispatch written by the major. The two walked backwards in their stocking feet so that their tracks would not readily give away their course of action. Within a few minutes they disappeared into the night.[45]

A diligent watch was kept up all night, but there were no further encounters with the Indians until dawn. When the sun came up, the warriors renewed their siege of the island. The Indians began the day with another charge, which was quickly repulsed by the scouts' carbines. Thoroughly rebuffed, the warriors positioned themselves around the island and initiated a continuous fire for the remainder of the day. The stronger fortifications built up on the island discouraged any further direct attack by the Indians, so there were few men wounded and none killed on the second day of the battle. The unrelenting sun, however, made life on the island doubly difficult. The intense sun putrified and bloated the dead animals, filling the air with a horrible stench. The wounded continued to suffer from want of medical supplies. That night, not knowing whether Stillwell and Trudeau had gotten away safely, Forsyth decided to send two more men for help. This time escape proved impossible, for the Indians had

A sweeping panoramic portrait of Beecher's Island Battlefield, with the postwar monument to the action visible in front of the clump of trees. *Brigham Young University*

blocked every avenue off the isolated island; the two men dispatched by Forsyth returned to their embattled comrades and awaited the coming of dawn.[46]

By the third day, it was apparent that the warriors had resolved on starving out the scouts. Realizing by now that charging the island was futile, the only shots fired were those of some Indian sharpshooters and the return fire of the scouts. As this exchange was going on, a handful of Indians carrying a white flag approached Forsyth's position in an apparent attempt to open communications with the scouts. Forsyth decided that this was a subterfuge to enable the Indians to retrieve the bodies of some of their comrades rather than an attempt to negotiate. He declined to meet the warriors. Grover, who could communicate with the Lakotas and Cheyenne, shouted out that they should not come near. However, the Indians continued to approach until several scouts opened fire on them.[47]

Because the scouts' only hope of survival was outside assistance, Forsyth decided to attempt a third time to send two men to Fort Wallace. John Donovan and A. J. Pliley were selected and were handed a dispatch written by Forsyth to the post commander, Col. Henry Bankhead. The message read:

ON DELAWARE CREEK, REPUBLICAN RIVER,
September 19, 1868[48]

To Colonel Bankhead, or Commanding Officer, Fort Wallace:

I sent you two messengers on the night of the 17th instant, informing you of my critical condition. I tried to send two more last night, but they did not succeed in passing the Indian pickets, and returned. If the others have not arrived, then hasten at once to my assistance. I have eight badly wounded and ten slightly wounded men to take in, and every animal I had was killed, save seven, which the Indians stampeded. Lieutenant Beecher is dead, and Acting Assistant Surgeon Moores probably cannot live the night out. He was hit in the head Thursday, and has spoken but one rational word since. I am wounded in two places—in the right thigh, and my left leg broken below the knee. The Cheyenne alone number 450 or more. Mr. Grover says they never fought so before. They were splendidly armed with Spencer and Henry rifles. We killed at least thirty-five of them, and wounded many more, besides killing and wounding a quantity of their stock. They carried off most of their killed during the night, but three of their men fell into our hands. I am on a little island, and have still plenty of ammunition left. We are living on mule and horse meat, and are entirely out of rations. If it was not for so many wounded, I would come in, and take the chances of whipping them if attacked. They are evidently sick of their bargain.

I had two of the members of my company killed on the 17th, namely, William Wilson and George W. Chalmers. You had better start with not less than seventy-five men, and bring all the wagons and ambulances you can spare. Bring a six-pound howitzer with you. I can hold out here for six days longer if absolutely necessary, but please lose no time.

Very respectfully, your obedient servant,

GEORGE A. FORSYTH,
U. S. Army, Commanding Co. Scouts.

P.S. My surgeon having been mortally wounded, none of my wounded have had their wounds dressed yet, so please bring out a surgeon with you.[49]

After the third day of the siege, most of the Indians withdrew. The several days following saw relatively little action.[50] However, the men were becoming increasingly desperate for food. During this lull, there was some talk among the healthy men of leaving to save their own lives. However, this would mean that they would have to abandon the wounded. When Forsyth learned of this development, he called the men together and asked them to delay an attempt to escape until the messengers had had time to summon help. He declared that if they would wait until then he would be willing to let them go. Hurst later said, "[Forsyth] talked so much like a brave soldier that there was not a murmur and I do not suppose one of the men could have been dared or induced to go under any circumstances." All would be saved together or all would die together.[51]

By the sixth day, September 22, the dried meat was gone. There had been a few attempts to spot and shoot game; still afraid that some war parties might be close by, the men dared not venture too far away to hunt. The only animal killed was a coyote, and it provided little meat. The scouts were left with only the decomposing and maggot-ridden carcasses of the dead animals. The stench was so great that the scouts could hardly stand being around the remains. However, in their desperation, the men cut off the best sections of flesh they could find and cooked them thoroughly in a fire. To deaden the rancid taste, they sprinkled gun powder on the meat as they cooked it, scraping it off before eating. This attempt at seasoning did little to improve the taste. At this time Chauncey B. Whitney penciled in his diary: "Still looking anxiously for relief. Starvation is staring us in the face; nothing but horse meat."[52]

The remaining days on the island seemed to last an eternity as the men waited and waited for relief to arrive. Some of the men began to find maggots infesting their cuts and bullet wounds. More serious suffering occurred as gangrene began to set in. Days seven and eight of the siege brought nothing but despair, hunger, and thoughts of death. As many of the men became convinced they were going to die, men were once again spotted advancing in their direction. The command was alerted in the fear that the Indians were preparing another attack, However, as the strangers approached, it became clear that they were members of the U.S. Army. Help had finally arrived after nine long days. Chauncey B. Whitney joyously recorded the rescue of September 25 in his diary:

> A day long to be remembered by our little band of heroes. Arose at daylight
> to feel all the horrors of starvation slowly but surely approaching. Got a light

John Donovan

Denver Public Library
Western History Department

breakfast on rotten meat. Some of the boys wandered away to find something to satisfy and appease their hunger. About ten o'clock the cry of Indians rang through the works. Some of the men being out, eight or ten of us took our guns to rescue them if possible. The word was given that it was friends. In a few moments, sure enough, our friends did come. Oh, the unspeakable joy! Shouts of joy and tears of gladness were freely commingled. Such a shaking of hands is seldom witnessed. Soon our hands were filled with something for the inner man, both in the shape of victuals and stimulants. The day passed off in joy and gladness among friends who condoled with us over our hardships and shouted for joy at our success against the enemy.[53]

Oddly, though Donovan and Pliley had been the second two men to leave for assistance and the second to arrive at Fort Wallace, they were the first to guide assistance to the island. After Donovan and Pliley had left the island on the third night of the battle, they had removed the

A. J. Pliley

Kansas State Historical
Society, Topeka, Kansas

moccasins from two dead warriors in hopes that this would make their tracks less discernible. Once they reached open prairie, cacti pierced through the soft leather footwear, swelling their feet to twice their normal size. Knowing that their comrades were depending on them, they nonetheless continued their journey despite the pain that shot up their legs with every step. The only food they had was some rotten horse flesh from the island. The pair finally arrived at a ranch house, where they obtained a ride to Fort Wallace by stagecoach.

As they entered Fort Wallace, they found that Stillwell and Trudeau had already reached the post. Colonel Bankhead, accompanied by Stillwell and Trudeau, had left with a relief column a short time earlier. Bankhead had also sent out a courier to find Col. Louis H. Carpenter, who was away on a road patrol, and to instruct him to also ride to Forsyth's rescue. Donovan set out to locate Carpenter and guide him to the island. Meanwhile, Pliley set out to find another cavalry detachment that was on patrol, that of Col. James Brisbane. All of these efforts resulted in three separate relief columns moving out to save Forsyth's scouts. By good fortune, Donovan quickly found Colonel Carpenter, who had with him Company H of the Tenth U.S. Cavalry, a regiment of the famed African-American "Buffalo Soldiers." Donovan led Carpenter's company directly to the island, which the soldiers reached on September 25.[54]

The adventures of Stillwell and Trudeau had been equally exciting. When they slipped away on the night of September 17, they passed closely by several small parties of Indians but were able to escape detection. Seeing that they were surrounded by enemies, the two chose to hide during the day and travel mainly by night. Several times they came to soft ground on which their boots left tracks. When confronted with this terrain, they walked backward so that the tracks would mislead any Indians who might spot their trail. At dawn on September 19, they found themselves on the edge of a large Indian camp. Fortunately, Stillwell and Trudeau were able to conceal themselves in a nearby marsh and escape detection.

At another point, after traveling all night, they sighted a party of Cheyenne warriors riding directly at them as dawn approached. The two men quickly crawled into the dead carcass of a large bull buffalo nearby. As they lay motionless, they noticed one warrior approach within a few yards of the bison. But just as they thought they would be discovered, the man turned and walked away. As the warrior was leaving, a rattlesnake appeared and seemed prepared to strike at the hidden scouts. A quick squirt of tobacco juice from Stillwell silenced the snake. On the evening of September 22, the two scouts finally reached Fort Wallace and alerted Colonel Bankhead, who immediately assembled a group of over 100 men from various units at the post and set out to rescue the trapped soldiers. Unfortunately, Bankhead refused to let Stillwell guide him. As a result, Bankhead arrived at the island on September 26, one day after Carpenter.[55]

For nine long, grueling days, Forsyth and his little company of fifty scouts held off several hundred Cheyenne, Arapaho, and Lakota Indians intent on taking their scalps. The majority of the men were wounded, and by the time of their rescue, the survivors were more dead than alive. The story of the engagement is one of tremendous bravery on both sides. The scouts fought courageously, and their survival was largely due to their quick decision to mount a defense from the island and to superior weapons. Had Forsyth decided to run on the first day of the attack, his command would certainly have been chased and annihilated by the large body of Indians. For the Cheyenne, the battle would have been just another minor incident except that the fight cost the life of one of their greatest warriors. Because of this, the Cheyenne called the battlefield "The Place Where Roman Nose Died." For soldiers and settlers, it became known as "Beecher Island Battlefield," in honor of the fallen Lt. Frederick H. Beecher.

The remarkable story of the scouts' survival quickly spread throughout the country as the army heralded it as a great example of courage and bravery. Due

Beecher Island monument erected by the states of Colorado and Kansas.

Reunion at Beecher's Island, in front of the monument.

Brigham Young University

to this, many of the scouts later wrote their personal accounts of the battle, and a memorial association was begun by and for the battle's veterans. In 1898, three of the scouts returned to the battle site and identified the location of the island. Soon afterwards a monument was erected to commemorate what had taken place. For many years, members of the memorial association returned to the scene. But as time passed and the veterans began passing away, periodic flooding destroyed the monument and the island, and the public soon forgot about this epic engagement.

The setbacks the Indians inflicted on Forsyth's and Sheridan's operations did them little good. If anything, the attack only helped inspire General Sheridan's decision to launch a winter campaign to punish the "hostiles" and force them to the reservations. For the Lakota, Cheyenne, and Arapaho, the battle remains primarily the event that cost themthe great warrior Roman Nose, who died trying to preserve their way of life.

NOTES

1. Thomas Ranahan, "What Caused the Beecher Island Fight," *The Beecher Island Annual* 5 (1917): 1-4; Donald J. Berthrong, *The Southern Cheyennes* (Norman: University of Oklahoma Press, 1963), 310.

2. General G. A. Forsyth, "A Frontier Fight." *Harpers New Monthly Magazine*, 91 (1895), 42.

3. Ibid.

4. John Hurst, "The Beecher Island Fight," *Kansas State Historical Society*, 15 (1919-1922), 530.

5. John Hurst interview, October 6, 1912, Walter Mason Camp Collection, Harold B. Lee Library, Brigham Young University, Provo (hereafter cited as Walter M. Camp Collection); Sigmund Schlesinger, "The Beecher Island Fight," *Kansas State Historical Society* 15 (1919-1922): 540; Forsyth, "A Frontier Fight, 42.

6. Forsyth, "A Frontier Fight," 42-43.

7. Ibid., 43.

8. Chauncey B. Whitney, "Diary of Chauncey B. Whitney," *Kansas State Historical Society* 12 (1911-1912): 296.

9. Schlesinger, "The Beecher Island Fight," 540;

10. Forsyth, "A Frontier Fight," 44; Whitney, "Diary of Chauncey B. Whitney," 296-297; The injured man had to be left behind and was replaced by Jim Curry. See Schlesinger, "The Beecher Island Fight," 541. There has been some question at to whether Jim Curry was with Forsyth because his name was not on the original monument. For further testimony that Jim Curry was with Forsyth after leaving Fort Wallace, see Walter M. Camp interviews of John Hurst, Sigmund Schlesinger, and James Peate, Walter M. Camp Collection.

11. Forsyth, "A Frontier Fight," 44; Hurst, "The Beecher Island Fight," 531.

12. Forsyth, "A Frontier Fight," 44-45.

13. Ibid., 45.

14. John Hurst interview, October 6, 1912, Walter M. Camp Collection.

15. John Hurst interview, October 6, 1912, and Eli Zigler interview, January 25, 1913, Walter M. Camp Collection; Forsyth, "A Frontier Fight," 45; Hurst, "The Beecher Island Fight," 531; Schlesinger, "The Beecher Island Fight," 542.

16. George E. Hyde, *Life of George Bent, Written From His Letters*, edited by Savoie Lottinville (Norman: University of Oklahoma Press, 1967), 298; George Bird Grinnell, *The Fighting Cheyenne* (Norman: University of Oklahoma Press, 1956), 281.

17. George Bent interview, Walter M. Camp Collection; Hyde, *Life of George Bent*, 298; Grinnell, *The Fighting Cheyenne*, 281.

18. Quoted from Stan Hoig, *The Peace Chiefs of the Cheyennes* (Norman: University of Oklahoma Press, 1980), 97; originally printed in Colonel James B. Fry, *Army Sacrifices* (New York: D. Van Nostrand, 1879).

19. Hyde, *Life of George Bent*, 306-307; Grinnell, *The Fighting Cheyennes*, 281.

20. Hyde, *Life of George Bent*, 307-308.

21. Ibid.; Grinnell, *The Fighting Cheyenne*, 287.

22. Hyde, *Life of George Bent*, 298-299; Grinnell, *The Fighting Cheyenne*, 282-283.

23. George Bent to Walter M. Camp, December 13, 1911, Walter M. Camp Collection. In this letter George Bent places the number of warriors with Starving Elk at about twenty. Yet, in Hyde's book *Life of George Bent*, which was written from the

letters of George Bent, the total number is placed at eight, a number with which Grinnell agrees. Hyde, 299; Grinnell, *The Fighting Cheyennes*, 283.

24. Hurst, "The Beecher Island Fight," 531-532.

25. Ibid., 531-532.

26. Forsyth, "A Frontier Fight," 47.

27. Eli Zigler interview, January 25, 1913, Walter M. Camp Collection.

28. Hurst, "The Beecher Island Fight," 532.

29. John Hurst interview, September 11, 1916, Walter M. Camp Collection; Hyde, *Life of George Bent*, 299-300. This island became the battlesite over the course of the next nine days. Though the island was later lost to flooding, its location is well known. It was located 16.5 miles southeast of present-day Wray, Colorado, on Beecher Road.

30. This story is told in John Hurst interview, September 11, 1916, Walter M. Camp Collection; also it is in Hurst, "The Beecher Island Fight," 535.

31. John Hurst interview, October 6, 1912, Walter M. Camp Collection.

32. Forsyth, "A Frontier Fight," 48-50; Hurst, "The Beecher Island Fight," 533; John Hurst interview, October 6, 1912, Walter M. Camp Collection.

33. In Forsyth's account he wrongly states that Roman Nose led the first charge of the day. It is very clear in Walter M. Camp's notes that the scouts on the island did not recognize Roman Nose at the time of the battle, and according to Camp, Roman Nose led the fifth and last charge of the day.

34. Hyde, *Life of George Bent*, 300-301; George Bent to Walter M. Camp, December 2, 1911 and December 13, 1911, Walter M. Camp Collection. Forsyth makes it sound as if many Indians were killed in this charge, but George Bent and Grinnell both say that none were killed. Forsyth, "A Frontier Fight," 48-49; Grinnell, *The Fighting Cheyennes*, 284.

35. Both Grinnell and George Bent say that Weasel Bear was the second Indian killed. Dry Throat had been killed when the Indians were circling the island. Grinnell, 284-285; Hyde, 301-302.

36. Grinnell, *Fighting Cheyennes*, 286; Hyde, *Life of George Bent*, 302.

37. Hurst, "The Beecher Island Fight," 534.

38. John Hurst interview, September 11, 1916, Walter M. Camp Collection.

39. Grinnell, *The Fighting Cheyenne*, 286.

40. Hyde, *Life of George Bent*, 302-303; Grinnell says that Roman Nose fell from his horse when he was hit. The warrior was then able to crawl up the bank, where some young men came and carried him away. Grinnell, *The Fighting Cheyennes*, 287-288. In Forsyth's account of the battle, "A Frontier Fight," he claims to have seen Roman Nose charge the island and be shot down. Forsyth also says that Roman Nose led the first great charge on the island. Several of the scouts later told Walter M. Camp that they did not recognize Roman Nose or hear of anyone who did until years after the battle. See Peate interview, January 18, 1913, and Sigmund Schlesinger interview, Walter M. Camp Collection.

41. Hyde, *Life of George Bent*, 303-304; Grinnell, *The Fighting Cheyennes*, 288-290.

42. Hurst, "The Beecher Island Battle," 535; Forsyth, "A Frontier Fight," 56.

43. Ibid.

44. John Hurst states that there was a tree above every pit and this meat was hung on it. John Hurst interview, October 6, 1912, and September 11, 1916, Walter M. Camp Collection; Forsyth, 57.

45. John Hurst interview, September 11, 1916, Walter M. Camp Collection. Hurst gives an interesting insight about Stillwell. He said: "I must frankly confess that this readiness of Stillwell to go on such a dangerous mission at once raised my estimate of him very much. He had been a gabby fellow, apparently careless in his ways and he was the man I least have expected to volunteer for such a dangerous mission. When he showed himself not only willing but eager to go I thought to myself that Stillwell after all was a much better man than I [had] ever taken him to be."

46. Forsyth, "A Frontier Fight," 58-59; Merrill J. Mattes, "The Beecher Island Battlefield Diary of Sigmund Schlesinger," *Colorado Magazine*, 29, 3 (July 1952): 169; Whitney, "Diary of Chauncey B. Whitney," 298.

47. Forsyth, "A Frontier Fight, 59; De B. Randolph Keim, *Sheridan's Troopers on the Borders: A Winter Campaign on the Plains*, (Glorieta, New Mexico: The Rio Grande Press, Inc., 1977, first published in 1870), 54. John Hurst mentions the white flag incident as he describes the first days events, Hurst, "The Beecher Island Fight," 535. Sigmund Schlesinger places the white flag incident on the second day, Mattes, 169.

48. It was actually the Arickaree Fork of the Republican River.

49. Forsyth, "A Frontier Fight," 59-60. Grinnell and George Bent both disagree with the number of killed that Forsyth reported and the kinds of weapons the Indians used. They say there were only nine Indians killed.

50. Hyde, *Life of George Bent*, 305; Grinnell, *The Fighting Cheyennes*, 291.

51. John Hurst interview, October 6, 1912, Walter M. Camp Collection.

52. Whitney, "The Diary of Chauncey B. Whitney," 298; Mattes, "The Beecher Island Battlefield Diary of Sigmund Schlesinger," 169; Hurst, "The Beecher Island Fight," 537.

53. Whitney, "The Diary of Chauncey B. Whitney," 298.

54. Alan W. Farley, ed., "Reminiscences of Allison J. Pliley Indian Fighter," *Trail Guide*, 2.2 (June 1957): 8-9. A. J. Pliley, "The Journey of Pliley and Donovan to Fort Wallace For Relief," *The Beecher Island Annual* 5 (1917), 42.

55. Winfield Freeman, "The Battle of Arickaree," *Transactions of the Kansas State Historical Society* 6 (1897-1900): 355-356; Lonnie J. White, *Hostiles and Horse Soldiers* (Boulder, Colorado: Pruett Publishing Company, 1972), 76.

Killing Ground

Forts of the West

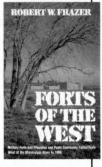

Military Forts and Presidios and Posts Commonly Called Forts West of the Mississippi River to 1898
By Robert W. Frazer

A systematic listing of all presidios and military forts which were ever, at any time and in any sense, so designated. The lists are arranged alphabetically within the boundaries of present states, and include for each fort: location, date and reason for establishment; name, rank, and military unit of the person establishing the post; present status or date of abandonment; and disposition of any existing military reservation. A map for each state shows the locations.
Paper, $14.95

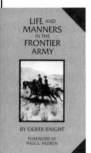

Life and Manners in the Frontier Army

By Oliver Knight
Foreword by Paul L. Hedren
"Persons seeking a true understanding of frontier military life will be well rewarded by reading *Life and Manners in the Frontier Army.*"—*North Dakota History*
Paper $15.95

Fort Laramie and the Great Sioux War

By Paul L. Hedren
Founded in 1834 in eastern Wyoming, Ft. Laramie evolved into an organizational hub and chief supply center for the U.S. Army in its campaigns against the Sioux and Cheyenne Indians. Hedren focuses on 1876—the year of General Crook's Big Horn, Yellowstone, and Powder River expeditions; the defeat of General Custer at the Little Big Horn; the Black Hills gold rush; and chaos at Indian agencies.
Paper, $15.95

The Arikara Narrative of Custer's Campaign and the Battle of the Little Bighorn

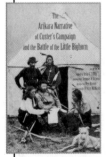

Edited by Orin G. Libby
Foreword by Jerome A. Greene, Preface by Dee Brown
Introduction by D'Arcy McNickle
Eyewitness reports on Custer's campaigns from 1874 through 1876, from the Indians who fought beside Custer—the Arikara scouts. Their accounts of the Battle of the Little Bighorn reveal much about why Custer failed—indeed, the Arikaras went into battle believing the Sioux medicine was so strong that defeat was inevitable.
Paper, $9.95

University of Oklahoma Press

4100 28th Avenue N.W. • Norman, OK 73069-8218
405.325.2000 or 800.627.7377 • Fax: 405.364.5798 or Fax: 800.735.0476
www.ou.edu/oupress • AMEX • Visa • MasterCard

A CONVERSATION
with Historian John H. Monnett

Interviewed by Jeff Broome

D r. John H. Monnett is a professor of history at Metropolitan State University in Denver, Colorado. He is the author of five books, the best celebrated to date being his works on the 1868 Battle of Beecher Island, Colorado, and the 1875 battle or battle-massacre at Sappa Creek, Kansas. Monnett became interested in the nineteenth century Plains Indians wars concurrently with his father's interest in the Civil War. (John's father, Howard Monnett, was the author of the definitive account of the Civil War Battle of Westport, Missouri.) In this interview, Dr. Monnett speaks of his findings on some of the most famous engagements on the central Plains. *JIW* is grateful to Dr. Jeff Broome for recording this fascinating conversation on current Indian wars study with one of the most original Indian wars scholars.

JB: John, what will you be covering in your upcoming book [Tell Them We're Going Home: The Odyssey of the Northern Cheyenne, 1878-1879 *(Norman, OK: University of Oklahoma Press, projected publication late 2000)]?*

JM: This book is the story of the famed exodus of the Northern Cheyenne who'd been sent to Indian Territory in 1878. Some of the Northern Cheyenne had participated in the Great Sioux War of 1876-1877. After they surrendered, the government decided to send the northerners to the [Oklahoma] Indian

Territory and concentrate them at the Darlington (Cheyenne-Arapaho) Indian Agency with the Southern Cheyenne. The Northern and the Southern Cheyenne were two distinct groups, but at this time the government was concentrating Indians of the same languages on the same reservations. This overtaxed the resources of the Cheyenne-Arapaho Reservation. Also, the northerners got homesick and were subject to malaria and other diseases of the south, diseases they hadn't know up north. The Northern Cheyenne chiefs Dull Knife and Little Wolf and their bands wanted to go home to Montana.

When the government refused their plea to return north, they left anyway and made an almost 2000-mile trek back to their homeland, fighting troops all through Kansas and up through Nebraska. The chiefs eventually separated. Dull Knife and his followers were captured and taken to Fort Robinson [Nebraska], where they then made a very famous and dramatic break out of Fort Robinson in January 1879. Most of them were killed. Little Wolf, on the other hand, actually made it up to Fort Keogh (Montana), surrendered there, and won his case at that point. His people were allowed to stay in the north. Dull Knife's and Little Wolf's is [the second of two] great, great Indian treks, the other being the flight of the Nez Perce Indians in 1877.

[*Tell Them We're Going Home*] is really the first complete . . . scholarly book on the subject. It's been done in pieces by other people through the years, [but] this is really the first composite non-fiction synthesis. Mari Sandoz' 1953 *Cheyenne Autumn* was a novel.

JB: When you began research on the Cheyenne trek back to Montana, your first move was to study primary sources. . . .

JM: Yes, and there's just a whole wealth of things to be found in the National Archives. The National Archives is loaded with materials. Concerning the Cheyenne outbreak, there were two investigations: one by the United States Congress and another by a board of officers at Fort Robinson. The officers were ordered there by General Crook, the commander of the Department of the Platte, who received orders from Washington to investigate what had happened. Some of the Indian prisoners gave testimony at these hearings, and their records are in the National Archives right along side the testimony of officers. . . .

JB: And isn't there an "Indian Depredations File" as well?

JM: Yes, there were a lot of civilian accounts [of Cheyenne depredations] from the counties the Cheyenne came through in Kansas. A lot of settlers filed claims with the state that were then sent to the Federal Government. . . .

JB: These claims can be very specific about certain acts that occurred and that sort of thing.

JM: Yes, there was one settler who filed for 25 cents for a lost book of matches. Another man filed a claim for $300 for a lost field of pumpkins. And there are all kinds of claims by women whose husbands were killed by the Indians. They put monetary values on their lives. There was one woman who valued her husband's life at $6,000, while her neighbor only asked for $4,000 for her husband. . . .

JB: Why did the Battle of Beecher Island (September 17-25, 1868) happen? [The battle is the subject of Dr. Monnett's The *Battle at Beecher Island and the Indian War of 1867-1869* (Niwot: University Press of Colorado, 1992) and one of his lifelong interests.]

JM: You have to keep in mind that at that time, 1868, most of the American military was in the South on [post-Civil War] Reconstruction duty. There was a general shortage of troops throughout the West. The Plains tribes were very much aware of that. You also had the lingering effects of the 1864 massacre of Black Kettle's Cheyenne at Sand Creek at that time. The Dog Soldiers [warrior society] in Kansas, eastern Colorado, and rest of the central Plains were still avenging Sand Creek. And right in the face of that, at the end of the Civil War, you had a tremendous migration of settlers coming out across the central Plains. Kansas' settlement quickly came from eastern Kansas out to about the 90th meridian. In a very steady fashion, the settlers went right through the lands of the Dog Soldiers.

The number one complaint of settlers during those years (1865-1868) was that there just weren't enough troops to protect them. . . . Fort Wallace was out there at the center of activity in western Kansas. But Fort Wallace was hopelessly isolated, with no railroad [connecting it to other forts], and hence you couldn't reinforce it. The fort was virtually under siege during the year 1867 and about half of 1868. It was probably the most besieged fort . . . on the Great Plains in the history of the Indian Wars. . . . The year 1867 was the bloodiest year in Kansas's history regarding Indian warfare. Casualties on both sides were high. When troops were put in the field . . . they could never catch up with the Indians. You know of Custer's experience in 1867, when he got his baptism of fire. He couldn't catch up to the Indians. Sheridan then came up with the idea of a swiftly moving ranger unit. He had done this in the Civil War with citizen soldiers, guerrillas essentially. Sheridan thought that a swiftly moving mobile force would be able to follow up any reported incident and at least keep the Indians on the move so that they wouldn't turn on the settlements.

JB: These rangers knew the Indians' ways?

JM: Some of them did, yes. They were settlers who lived right on the frontier line. They were good shots and good horsemen. Unfortunately, Sheridan's idea didn't work. It was the Indians who immobilized the scouts [at Beecher Island]. And that was the first and last time Sheridan ever used such a concept on the Plains.

JB: What significance do you think that the Battle of Beecher Island had in Indian warfare?

JM: I think its importance is how it captured the public imagination in years after. . . . The battle portrayed the idea of a successful defensive stand. Of course, when you juxtapose that against things like Little Bighorn and the Fetterman Fight, which were unsuccessful, [George] Forsyth and his scouts kind of became latter day heroes . . . . We look back on the Indian Wars, at all these defensive stands that stood out in the history, and here was one where the whites essentially survived. Other than that it really doesn't have much significance, especially for the Cheyenne and Lakotas.

JB: In terms of being outnumbered, "x" amount of Indians per white man so to speak, the odds were equal to the Fetterman and Custer battle, and yet these men at Beecher Island pulled through.

JM: Yes. They had several things going for them, of course. They had superior firepower by all accounts. They had seven-shot Spencer rifles, and they were able to make a defensive stand on a low point of ground rather than on a high point where they would have been exposed. . . . They were dug in, and the

Cheyenne were very much noted for not wanting to take unnecessary casualties. If it wasn't going to be an easy victory, they would lose interest, which they did here. From their point of view, it's just as subtle and non-dramatic as that.

JB: You perform research, you write these books, and you have a passion for this. Is there anything that sticks out about the Beecher Island fight that really touches you as a human interest story?

JM: I think what stands out in my mind is the death of the Cheyenne warrior, Roman Nose. Whether it was wish fulfillment or not, we'll never know, but he predicted his own death at that battle. He had a [violation of] his "medicine" that foretold his own death. He had eaten food with an unconsecrated utensil, which was a taboo. He said if he went into battle, he would die. And he did. What has stuck in my mind is the description of his burial. It comes to us through George Bird Grinnell from the Cheyenne. Roman Nose's wife and family took him down one of the forks of the Republican River and buried him on a scaffold in the traditional manner. There are all kinds of stories that came out later when the relief forces looking for Forsyth came through, they found a scaffold burial of an important warrior and they desecrated it. But, according to my research, by all accounts it wasn't Roman Nose. . . .

[After] some further investigation as to where his grave would be today, as close as I can pinpoint, it's right smack dab in the middle of Burlington Reservoir in eastern Colorado. It's under about twenty feet of water.

JB: Your most recently published book is entitled Massacre at Cheyenne Hole: Lieutenant Austin Henely and the Sappa Creek Controversy *(Niwot: University Press of Colorado, 1999). What drew your interest to this battle?* [Note: The April 23, 1875, Battle of Sappa Creek took place during a Cheyenne flight from Indian Territory two years before the unrelated flight of Dull Knife's Cheyenne band.]

JM: It's a very obscure incident, really. As I delve more and more into the Indian Wars in Kansas, I realize how little has been written. With Sappa Creek, there was something ripe for interpretation. Unfortunately, right in the middle of my research William Chalfant came out with a book on the subject. . . . His is a very fine book, so consequently I reshaped mine. . . . I realized that Sappa

Creek was the incident that [affected] how we viewed the Indian Wars from the time they were going on right down to the present day. The interpretation of what happened at Sappa Creek has changed 180 degrees and back again over the course of more than a century.

JB: What do you mean?

JM: I'll describe the battle very briefly in order to get to that. At the end of the Red River War, after the Sand Hill Fight [north of the Darlington Agency, in the Indian Territory], many Southern Cheyenne broke from the reservation and decided to head north to join with relatives and friends among the Northern Cheyenne. . . . They had to come through the Kansas settlements. But unlike the late 1860s, the military at this time was well equipped to converge on them. The railroads had connected Fort Lyon (Colorado) with Ft. Wallace, for example. The military, of course, wanted to keep the Indians away from the settlements.

One group of Southern Cheyenne, under Little Bull . . . were on their way to Montana but stopped to lay over on Sappa Creek in Northern Kansas, in the Republican River valley. . . . This area was in the rich buffalo zone, and was one of the last areas to be settled by advancing white civilization. . . . Little Bull and his people, camped on Sappa Creek, thought they were safe under a bluff. Henely's soldiers from Ft. Lyon had quickly come by rail to Ft. Wallace and from there picked up the [Cheyenne] trail . . . mostly with the help of a . . . post trader at Fort Wallace. . . Henely led a surprise attack at dawn. The Indians were taken by complete surprise.

JB: How many Indians are we talking about?

JM: Henely's report states that twenty-seven Indians were killed, nineteen of them warriors and the other eight being women and children. This was maybe sixty percent of the Indians. I'd say 30 to 40 percent of the Indians made their way to their horses and escaped [and] the rest were killed. . . . Henely was given a hero's accord when he ended the campaign and got back to Ft. Lyon. Several of his men were awarded the Medal of Honor.

JB: The earliest interpretation was that it was a heroic act.

JM: Right, and Henely's account is very straightforward. But in later years, one of his men turned on him and came out with a different story, one that claimed that atrocities had been committed, that wounded Cheyenne were killed after the fighting had ended. Henely burned the village and all supplies, which was common practice in the military. You wanted to deprive the enemy of resources. . . . Later there were allegations that wounded Cheyenne were thrown into the fire. One sergeant many years later came up with the story that a baby, an infant, who was very much alive, was tossed into a teepee, and the teepee caught on fire. The numbers, of course, have escalated over the years.

No atrocity stories came out prior to 1907. Then a settler by the name of William Street claimed to have been told of atrocities by one of the buffalo hunters that happened to be there. Street came up with the claim that living people had been consumed by fire at the end of the battle. Another settler, Frank Lockhard, who also lived in the region, supported Street's story with pretty much the same claim a year later. It's never really been substantiated. It could have happened, but there's always going to be a doubt about it. In any event, some attitudes regarding Indian people changed in America by the first decade of the twentieth century. This reflected some of the changing social attitudes during the so-called progressive movement, during the decade and a half from the Theodore Roosevelt administration down to World War I.

JB: And you had Wounded Knee, too.

JM: Right, this controversy developed in the wake of the Wounded Knee massacre of 1890. Attitudes were changing, and whether or not some of these stories that came out were from people who . . . had withheld telling the truth at an earlier time . . . or whether these guys were just capitalizing on the moods of [the progressive] era, we will never really know. . . .

The real shocker is the testimony of George Bent, whose accounts did not come to light until 1964. . . . George Bent was the mixed-blood son of William Bent and Owl Woman. . . . He had been at Sand Creek, and after that time disavowed the white side of his family and rode with the Dog Soldiers. Eventually he went to the reservation with the Southern Cheyenne and, as an old man in the early twentieth century, being literate, wrote many letters to George Hyde, the anthropologist, about his reminiscences of the Indian Wars and his interviews with other warriors. . . . Hyde organized all these letters over the years that George Bent had written to him of his reminiscences into a manuscript, *The Life of George Bent*. . . . Hyde donated it to the Denver Public Library, where it was forgotten and gathered dust on a shelf until 1964. . . Here is one of the most important Southern Cheyenne accounts of this period, covering the time from the 1840s through the 1870s.

JB: And Bent adds to the interpretation of Sappa Creek?

JM: Yes, his last few paragraphs are on the Sappa Creek fight. Essentially what Bent comes out with is that the Cheyenne under Little Bull did try to surrender. They came out under a flag of truce. That collaborates some of the early white accounts. According to George Bent, one Cheyenne warrior fired on the two soldiers who came out to receive the truce pardon. The soldiers, of course, became swept away with fury. This sealed the fate of Little Bull's Southern Cheyenne. So Bent places the reason for the massacre, if there was a massacre—which by all accounts I think there was—as being brought on in retaliation for the actions of this one warrior. . .

JB: With one impetuous warrior who wouldn't agree to negotiation . . .

JM: That's what Bent claimed. I know that may not be popular among the Cheyenne. . . . You have to look at . . . all the different accounts. When you put Bent's together with Henley's records and some of the others, you can see events in a more complete light. . . . What happened after the fight is a real mystery—we'll never know. I think the importance of the incident is how its interpretation has changed to reflect the mood of the times, right down to the present day. . . .

JB: To what extent has the Sappa Creek Massacre been affected by what you call "the context of evolving intellectual and political attitudes through the years?" How does the modern historian avoid falling into this trap in understanding history?

JM: I think you're going to be in that trap. It's how you get out of it that is significant. I think any historian has to understand up front that all history to some degree is political. . . . My big complaint, and I have the same complaint about . . . "Old Western historians" in this regard as I do "New Western historians," is that [they fail to] examine both sides, or all sides, of the conflict.

When you're dealing with an historical event that is a conflict situation, you have to examine both sides from the point of view of each side. Old Western historians have traditionally only presented the Euro-American side of the story. Then came a new wave of Indian histories. It was very biased in the Indian direction with very little balance. Then, with the New Western History, there's been a total rejection of the Indian Wars as being nothing other than part of blanket global imperialism.

JB: On page 106 of your Sappa Creek book, you describe your perspective as a "realist" perspective in understanding history. . . . Tell us a little bit what you mean by that.

JM: I think you have to look at both sides, again, of the conflict without trying to be judgmental. So often, and I think this comes from the traditional formulaic way to look at Western history and its conflicts, we see good guys and bad guys, heroes in white hats and villains in black hats. Whenever we revise our history, we say "Okay, who are the guys in white hats this year, and who are the guys in black hats this year? Are they different from last year?" I don't think you can get a good accurate picture of what went on; you can't get an understanding of what went on if you keep seeking simple explanations defined in terms of composite victims and victimizers.

You have to start with the mentality that you simply have people . . . acting within the context of their own culture. How these people deviate from the norms of their own culture defines what is good versus evil. I think in the West you have a history of extremely diverse cultures, each with different visions of how the land should be utilized in the future. In some cases, their . . . visions are incompatible, say as in large-scale agriculture versus [preservation of] an expansive buffalo range. The failure of all these cultures to compromise their vision brought about conflict because compromise meant modifications would affect their future affluence. In some cases there was a "winner take all" mentality. . . . This is nothing unique, it's nothing peculiarly "Western."

Before you place blame, you have to look at the context of the times. I'll be the first to say that, in many respects, you can still place blame even within the context of that past era. But don't do it by the context of the twenty-first century. That's called "presentism." If you're looking for understanding of the event . . . not just the facts but the motivations behind the event, you've got to go beyond that point.

JB: You've written, for example, about the [John] German family massacre of autumn, 1874, and its contribution to the Sappa Creek fight. On page 29 of the Sappa Creek book you mentioned Catherine German, the young teenaged girl, having been "put on the prairie." This was a Cheyenne practice. Would you explain that as a cultural practice?

JM: It was essentially a practice of [punitive] gang rape that was done by warrior societies . . . Cheyenne women were very noted for their chastity, and therefore it was a tremendous offense when they were unchaste. On occasion it was the option of the husband, if the wife had been unfaithful, to "put her on the prairie." He would allow all the members of his warrior society to paint her, put her on a horse, take her out of the village, and descend on her and gang rape her. When the Cheyenne began their wars with the whites, this practice was directed against their white enemies. To paraphrase Father Peter John Powell, the renowned Cheyenne historian, whites were the enemies of the people, and their captive women sometimes were treated like unchaste Cheyenne women. . . . It was an act of indignity done because whites were the enemy. They'd come to take [the Cheyenne] lands, their buffalo.

JB: Practices like this were in turn hardening the Euro-American perspective. The soldiers were aware of [what had happened to the Germans and others] and knew, because they had been identified prior to their escape from the reservation, that it had been carried out by Indians like those at Sappa Creek.

JM: [Because we] shape stereotypes in the context of our own culture today, [it's difficult for us to] understand things like this in the context of those times.

JB: You earlier mentioned Mari Sandoz and her novel, Cheyenne Autumn. *Can you talk about that book?*

JM: I haven't been able to avoid Mari Sandoz in writing both the Sappa Creek book and my newest, on the Northern Cheyenne exodus from Indian Territory in 1878, because they're very much intertwined. It has been accepted for years that depredations committed by Little Wolf, and Dull Knife's people when they came north through Kansas in 1878 were in revenge for the Sappa

Creek Massacre. This is because the settlers they descended on were living right in the same area where Henely attacked Little Bull's camp in 1875. Through my research on both topics, I have to very much disagree with Mari Sandoz's support of this conclusion. For one thing, one of the reasons the Northern Cheyenne came north in 1878 was because they weren't accepted socially by the Southern Cheyenne on the reservation. . . . There was a lot of animosity. Now if you left the reservation for that reason, why would you want to jeopardize your trip north by avenging a massacre of the Southern Cheyenne people who kicked you off their reservation? I don't buy it.

Investigating further, going through virtually all of Mari Sandoz's papers at the University of Nebraska, what I found was that her claim that the Dull Knife raids in Kansas were in revenge for the Sappa Creek Massacre were all based on the Street and Lockhard accounts written back in 1908 and 1909. . . . Street's is the only one, the only place, the only quasi-contemporary source, that states "it has always seemed to me, that the Dull Knife raids in 1878 was somehow connected to the Sappa Creek event." Sandoz undoubtedly picked up on that word "somehow," and made the claim that indeed it was so. She infers that she talked to Cheyenne about this, . . . but she certainly didn't have any substantive sources other than Street and Lockhard.

Now, once you put the whole Cheyenne odyssey of 1878-1879 together, you realize that a few days before the Cheyenne came into the northern Kansas settlements, they suffered almost the complete destruction of their spare horses at the Battle of Punished Woman's Fork (September 27, 1878) near Scott City, Kansas. They had lost all of their pack horses and their provisions of dried meat from cattle that they had killed in southwestern Kansas. Cheyenne success depended upon staying ahead of the army constantly with fresh horses for women, children, and old people. After the Battle of Punished Woman's Fork, they came into the settlements, and they needed horses. . . . They came away with some 200 of them. Naturally, white settlers are going to shoot back, defend their property, and that would be what I found actually happened. [The attacks were motivated more by] a desperate need for resources at that point, I think, than any kind of revenge. . . .

JB: Do you have any ideas why the Medicine Lodge Treaty of 1867 failed?

[Note: In the treaty negotiated on Medicine Lodge Creek, Kansas, some representatives of the Southern Cheyenne, Southern Arapahos, and other Plains peoples signed an agreement pleading that their nations would settle upon the Indian Reservation in present-day Oklahoma. Raids in Kansas and Nebraska in 1868, the flight north from Indian Territory by Little Bull's band in 1875, and the similar exodus by Dull Knife's and Little Wolf's bands in 1878-1879 were all viewed as violations of the treaty, which resulted in the military actions described in this interview.]

JM: It's simple, actually. This was, as I understand it, the only treaty that the government actually got some of the Dog Soldier [warrior society] chiefs to sign. The Dog Soldiers were the critical factor among the Southern Cheyenne in terms of danger to the settlements of the central Plains. Whether they understood what they were signing or not has been debated. But in any event, the next spring, that of 1868, a huge war party of Dog Soldiers left the Indian Territory figuring, "Well, this treaty with the United States had to do with a conflict between us and the whites, but it doesn't have anything to do with the Pawnees." So they went out to make a big raid on the Pawnees. They came across a line of white settlements in the Saline River valley. A number of young Dog Soldier warriors, wanting to avenge a death of a relative or a friend [at the hands of whites], found too much temptation. They descended on some of the settlements along White Rock Creek, the Saline River, and the Solomon River and that started warfare again. [These streams were part of the watershed of Nebraska and Kansas's Republican River watershed.] The Dog Soldiers from that point on said, "We're never going to surrender our Republican River valley. They headed north to the valley after the great Saline and Solomon raids and pledged to stay there and never go back to the reservation. That buried the Treaty of Medicine Lodge as far as Dog Soldiers were concerned. . . .

Matters were made worse by the fact that the Cheyenne and Arapaho reservation established under the Medicine Lodge Treaty was at Darlington Agency [a poor location] in the Indian Territory. Then the government made matters worse by moving some of the Northern Cheyenne there. The northerners, who were by this time more closely associated with the Lakotas with than the Southern Cheyenne, were in some cases resented by the southerners when resources became scarce. So the northerners left for the Lakota agencies up north. . . . The Northern Cheyenne could by a treaty stipulation attach themselves to one of the Lakota ["Sioux"] Indian agencies—Red Cloud, and eventually Pine Ridge—or to the Shoshone Indian reservation in Wyoming.

JB: That treaty was the one that ended the [Bozeman Trail War], the Treaty of Fort Laramie (1868)?

JM: Right. The Northern Cheyenne took that to mean that they had a treaty with the federal government, but they really didn't. They were just kind of a footnote to the Lakota treaty [i.e., the Treaty of Fort Laramie]. The Northern Cheyenne never had a distinct treaty with the United States. But nonetheless, they were allowed to continue to live in the North. That would cause them all kinds of trouble from 1868 right down to 1879 because . . . Northern Cheyenne and Southern Cheyenne . . . had relatives in both camps. Southern Cheyenne would constantly go north to see relatives, northerners would come south. They come right through the central plains in Kansas and Nebraska.

That's where trouble started. The frontier line—and I believe there were distinct frontier lines, at least in Kansas during the late 1870's—was right at the 100th meridian. There was settlement on one side [of the meridian], buffalo range on the other. The Cheyenne would come up the western side of the settlements as they went going back and forth to visit each other. Then white settlement expanded further westward. . . .

Troubles were guaranteed to ensue when the central Plains also became the escape route used by Indians during the Red River War of 1874-1875. A lot of Southern Cheyenne wanting to escape that war were going north via this route. For example, Stone Forehead, the keeper of the Cheyenne Sacred Arrows, took the arrows up to the Northern Cheyenne people in 1875 so that they wouldn't be taken by the whites.

The government consequently made the mistake in 1877 of saying, "All right, to end traffic through the settlements between the Northern and Southern Cheyenne, take the northern people and make them move them down to Darlington Agency in the south. . . ." That only made matters worse by making conditions more intolerable on the reservation.

JB: So, the Treaty of Medicine Lodge failed almost immediately because of the resistance of the Dog Soldiers?

JM: But it continued to fail for all these other reasons for a decade afterwards. I think, in closing, that if the Indian wars proved anything, they proved that largely one-sided treaties could never [reconcile] the incompatible visions of the future held by whites and Indians or compensate for the emotional loss of their visions by the losers.

JB: Thank you for your time.

JM: You're welcome.

AMERICAN INDIAN HISTORY

Phil Konstantin

With this issue, *JIW* welcomes a new columnist, Phi Konstantin. Phil will be familiar to many of our readers as the creator of the widely recognized website "On This Date in American Indian History." Besides the featured "On This Date" section, the site contains one of the largest sets of links to American Indian resources on the internet (http://americanindian.net).

A graduate of Rice University, Phil has been a longtime amateur historian. He has written over 100 magazine and newspaper articles on various subjects and is the author of an upcoming book from Savas Publishing based on his "On This Date in American Indian History" concept. Phil is a California Highway Patrol officer and once served as a NASA Mission Control computer operator. Phil's registered tribal membership is in the Cherokee nation of Oklahoma.

Beginning with the next issue, Phil will identify major events that took place in the months corresponding to our next quarter year of publication. As a sample of his website and future columns, Phil below provides information on events corresponding to the past two months. This time he has chosen events relevant to the Cheyenne nation, a major topic of several articles in this issue.

Cheyenne Indians in May and June

May 16, 1864: After the negotiation of a treaty at Fort Wise [Colorado], the Cheyenne thought they would be able to continued hunting in their old hunting grounds if they lived in an area bounded by the Arkansas River and Sand Creek. However, what they were told was in the treaty and what was really stated in it was considerably different. While on a routine hunting trip near Ash Creek [Kansas], Black Kettle, Lean Bear, and others hear of a group of soldiers approaching their camp. On this date, Lean Bear and a small party ride out to see the soldiers. Lean Bear had visited Washington the year before and been presented medals and certificates stating he was a "good Indian." Carrying these credentials, Lean Bear approaches the troops. When he is about 100 feet from the soldiers, they open fire, and Lean Bear is killed. The soldiers then direct their fire against Lean Bear's entire party. The Indians begin to fight back.

As more Indians ride in from their camp, the army responds with grapeshot from their cannons. Black Kettle responds by urging the Indians to stop fighting. Eventually the Indians cease shooting, and the soldiers retreat. The cavalrymen, led by Lieutenant George Eayre, were members of Colonel John M. Chivington's Colorado volunteer regiment (of later Sand Creek Massacre infamy); the soldiers had been operating outside of their jurisdiction.

May 16, 1869: Lieutenant William Volkmar of the Fifth U.S. Cavalry was leading advance troops of General Asa Carr's command, seeking to find Indian survivors of the May 13 fight at Beaver Creek, Kansas. On May 16, Volkmar finally catches up to the Indians at Spring Creek in Nebraska. According to his report, Volkmar's patrol is attacked by approximately 400 warriors. Fighting from behind the corpses of their dead horses, the troops are able to hold off the Indians until General Carr's main body arrives. The column chases the Indians for almost fifteen miles to the Republic River, where the Indians split up into small groups. General Carr believes the warriors to be members of the Cheyenne Dog Soldier warrior society. The army will issue a Congressional Medal of Honor to First Lieutenant John B. Babcock for his exploits in the fight.

June 26, 1874: Comanches under Quanah Parker decided to punish white hunters for killing their buffalo herds and taking their grazing lands. Joined by Kiowas, Southern Cheyenne, and Southern Arapaho, they set out for a trading post at a place called Adobe Walls in the Panhandle of Texas. The Comanche "medicine man" [shaman] Isatai promises that the bullets of the white men will not harm them. A buffalo hunter named Billy Dixon sees the Indians approaching and is able to fire a warning shot before the attack. The Indians charge the trading post, occupied by twenty-eight men and one woman. The buffalo hunters there have very accurate, long-range rifles with telescopic sights. Dixon reportedly knocks an Indian off his horse from 1,538 yards away with one of these rifles. The post's sod walls provide very good cover. Slightly more than a dozen Indians will be killed in the fight, and Isatai will be humiliated. The Indians give up the fight as hopeless and leave. Some sources report the date of this fight as June 27, 1874, and/or report it lasting until July 1.

THE FIRST CONGRESSIONAL
Medal of Honor for a Buffalo Soldier

Patrick A. Bowmaster

I set the Spencers [cavalry carbines] to talking and whistling about their ears so lively that they broke in confusion and fled to the hills leaving us their herd of five horse," wrote the brave and formidable Sergeant Emanuel Stance of the Ninth U.S. Cavalry. The words are from his report of the scouting experience that earned him the first Congressional Medal of Honor ever awarded to a black-American in the United States Regular Army. The decoration was the high point of the military career of an unsung individual who, although deeply flawed, should be recognized as an American hero.

Emanuel Stance's military career began in 1866 when the nineteen-year-old Carroll Parish, Louisiana native enlisted in the Ninth U.S. Cavalry. The Ninth Cavalry regiment was one of the six United States regiments organized after the Civil War that were to be manned by black enlistees. Such recruits would come be to known as the "Buffalo Soldiers," after admiring Indians compared their hair, complexion, endurance, and fortitude to that of bison.

Evidence suggests that Stance was likely a slave before emancipation and a sharecropper immediately after. He probably became a Buffalo Soldier for the same reasons that other African-Americans of the period did: the military offered steady employment, near professional equality with whites, and a chance to begin a new life out West.

Stance spent the last four and a half years of his new life in the army on the Western frontier in the Department of Texas. There he participated in several Indian fights and was promoted to corporal and then sergeant in Company F of the Ninth Cavalry. During his first five-year enlistment period, a portion of Stance's company was ordered out from Fort McKavett on May 19, 1870, on a punitive scout. The company captain, Henry Carroll, wanted to punish the Mescalero Apache Indians for depredations against area settlers. Raiding was a central part of the Apache culture. This exasperated the tensions that unavoidably developed between the Indians and U.S. citizens in competition for available resources. Conflict between the two groups had been ongoing and would continue until the last Apache bands were permanently confined to reservations. The most recent provocations included the Apache kidnapping of two children from a family in Texas' Loyal Valley. In response, Carroll led his men out in pursuit of the offending warriors.[1]

Stance led an independent detachment of troopers during the scout. The following is Stance's report of the role of his detachment:

Fort McKavett, Texas   May 26, 1870
[To] [Second] Lieutenant B. M. Custer
Post Adjutant

Lieutenant:

I have the honor to make the following report of a scout after Indians made in compliance with Special Orders No 73 [words illegible] Headquarters Post at Fort McKavett, Texas, May 19, [18]70.

I left camp on the 20th of May taking the Kickapoo road. When some fourteen (14) miles out I discovered a party of Indians making across the hills having a herd of [stolen] horses with them. I charged them and after slight skirmishing they abandoned the herd and took to the mountains. Having secured the horses—9 in number—I resumed my march to Kickapoo Springs and camped for the night. The following morning, I decided to return to the Post with my captured stock as they would embarrass further operations as my command was small numbering ten all told. I accordingly started about 6 o'clock A.M. When about ten miles from Kickapoo, I discovered a party of Indians about 20 in number making for a couple of Government teams which were about three miles in advance of us. They evidently meant to capture the stock as there was only a small guard

with the teams. I immediately attacked them by charging them. They tried hard to make a stand to get their herd of horses off but I set the Spencers [carbines] to talking and whistling about their ears so lively that they broke in confusion and fled to the hills leaving us their herd of five horses.
Resuming the march toward Camp they skirmished along my left flank to the right [words illegible] evidently being determined to take the stock[.] I turned my little command loose on them at this place and after a few volleys they left me to continue my march in peace. I reached camp at 2 P.M. on the 21st with 15 head of horses captured from the Indians.

The casualties of this scout was one horse slightly wounded.

I have the honor to be Very respectfully
Your Ob[edien]t. Servant
Emanuel Stance
Sergeant Co[mpany]"F" 9[th] Cavalry[2]

Sergeant Stance's detachment reportedly wounded four Apaches while suffering no casualties of their own.[3] Unknown to Stance, his charge in the skirmish on May 20 allowed one of the kidnapped boys to escape. The child, Willie Buckmeier, had been thrown free of a horse shared with an Apache warrior when the Indian fled from Stance's men. The boy reached the safety of a stage station at Kickapoo Springs the next day.

Captain Carroll attached an endorsement to Stance's report before it was forwarded to Colonel Edward Hatch at military subdistrict headquarters at Fort Davis:

Headquarters Fort McKavett, Texas
June 1, 1870

Respectfully forwarded to H[ea]d. Q[uarters]. Sub. Dist[rict]. of the Pecos. The gallantry displayed by the Sergeant and his party as well as good judgment used on both occasions deserves much praise. As this is the fourth and fifth encounter that Sgt. Stance has had with Indians within the past two years on all of which occasions he has been mentioned for good behavior by his immediate Commanding Officer it is a pleasure to commend him to higher authority.

Henry Carroll
Captain 9th Cavalry
Commanding Post[4]

Carroll's commendation of Stance "to higher authority" included the recommendation that Stance receive the Congressional Medal of Honor. As a result, Stance received the award and was decorated with it on July 24, 1870. The sergeant was the first black-American to win the distinction in the post-Civil War period. Perhaps more significantly, he was the first black soldier in the Regular Army [i.e., the federal, professional army] to ever win the decoration.

Stance expressed his appreciation for the award in a letter to the adjutant general of the U.S. Army, who was at that time Brigadier General E. D. Townsend:

> Fort McKavett Texas
> July 24, 1870
>
> To The Adjutant General United States Army
> Washington D.C.
>
> General: I have the honor to acknowledge the receipt of a Communication of July 9, 1870 from the Adjutant Generals Office Enclosing Medal of Honor. I will cherish the gift as a thing of priceless value and endeavor by my future conduct to merit the high honor conferred upon me.
>
> I have the honor to be Very Respectfully
> Your Obedient Servant
> Emanuel Stance Sergeant F Co. 9t[h] Cav[alry][5]

Stance did do much "to merit the high honor conferred upon" him while serving in New Mexico Territory, Colorado Territory, and Nebraska during the following seventeen years of his military career. During these years, in which his company saw substantial combat with Indians, the army officially commended his martial character on three occasions. Stance rose to the rank of first sergeant [i.e., the senior sergeant of a company) and was appointed color sergeant [the sergeant with the honor of carrying a unit's flag on parade].

Yet Stance's service between 1870 and 1887 also revealed him to be a person who was far from perfect. Five different times he lost his non-commissioned officer rank and was reduced to being a private for failure to perform his duty. Stance suffered a loss of pay and served a six-month confinement at hard labor after having been caught drunk while on duty, having threatened the soldier who had found him intoxicated, and having attacked this same soldier and bitten off part of the man's lower lip. More seriously, Stance allegedly enforced an abusive brand of discipline upon those serving under him.

It was presumably this conduct which motivated one or more of his subordinates to murder him on Christmas Eve, 1887. Four days after the killing, the army buried Stance in the post cemetery at Fort Robinson, Nebraska. The military honors he received at his funeral represented the closing scene of the lengthy and conspicuous military career of a top-notch military man.

Unfortunately, Emanuel Stance has been forgotten by all except a group of present-day Buffalo Soldier scholars and by those who have read the few published details of his life drawn from scant primary sources. Still, Sergeant Stance deserves to be remembered as an individual who was able to slip through the cracks of the institutional racism of the nineteenth-century United States and earn a place as an inspiring, though imperfect, figure.[6]

NOTES

1. Henry Carroll enlisted in the Third U.S. Artillery Regiment in 1859 and became second lieutenant in that unit. Following the Civil War, he was promoted to the rank of captain in the Ninth Cavalry (1867). In 1890 he received brevet promotion to major in recognition of his conduct in two skirmishes with the Indians in 1869 and 1880. The latter skirmish left him severely wounded. He later became a full major in the First Cavalry and lieutenant colonel of the Sixth Cavalry. Carroll temporarily left the Regular Army in 1898 to serve as a brigadier general of state volunteers during the Spanish-American War. After his return to the Regulars, he became colonel of the Seventh Cavalry in 1899 but retired soon thereafter.

2. Emanuel Stance to B. M. Custer, May 26, 1870, RG 94, Letters Received by the Adjutant and Inspector General's Office, 1861-1870, National Archives, Washington, D.C.

The recipient of the report, B. M. Custer, enlisted in the Nineteenth Pennsylvania Volunteer Infantry Regiment when the American Civil War began in 1861. He later served in the Ninetieth Pennsylvania Infantry and Thirty-second U.S. Colored Infantry, becoming a lieutenant in the latter unit. Custer entered the Regular Army after the Civil War and spent the remained of his career in the Eleventh U.S. Colored Infantry, the Thirty-eighth Infantry, and the Eleventh Infantry regiments.

He received a brevet promotion for gallantry during that career and rose to the rank of captain before dying in 1887.

3. Adjutant General's Office, *Chronological List of Actions, &c., with Indians, from January 1, 1866, to January, 1891* (Washington, D.C.: U.S. Army, n.d.), 23.

4. Henry Carroll to [Head Quarters Subdistrict of the Pecos], June 1, 1870, ibid.

5. Emanuel Stance to Adjutant General, United States Army, July 24, 1870, ibid.

6. For more on Stance, see Patrick A. Bowmaster, "Westerners: Emanuel Stance," *Wild West*, February 1997, 32, 34, and Frank N. Schubert, *Black Valor: Buffalo Soldiers and the Medal of Honor, 1870-1898* (Wilmington: SR Books, 1997), 9-26.

THE INDIAN WARS

Battlefield, Tribal, Preservation, and Museum News

This column is reserved for news of archaeology and preservation, reenactments and commemorations, organizational and educational events, art exhibits, and tribal events. We welcome letters, news letters, clippings, and press releases. Brief extracts are more likely to be published.

Indians and WWII: Two distinguished Indian warriors of World War II were honored this year. Alexander H. Matthews, former president of the Pawnee Nation, was the first member of that nation to experience combat in the conflict. Matthews' was the last American unit to surrender with the fall of Corregidor and Baatan in the Phillipines, and he is a survivor of the infamous Bataan death march. In April, he was awarded a long overdue Bronze Star and eleven other citations and recognitions in a ceremony in Santa Fe.

In the same week, Charles Chibitty was recognized with a ceremonial honor dance at the Comanche Community Center in Apache, Oklahoma. Chibitty is the last surviving member of the Comanche code talker unit stationed in the European theater. Like the better known Navajo code talker units, the Comanche group used its own language to transmit encoded battlefield messages. Chibitty also recently received the Knowlton Award in Washington, D.C. for his patriotism and wartime service. Both men are members of their tribes' Indian veterans associations, groups which continue the heritage of historic warrior societies. (Source: *Oklahoma Indian Times*, May, 2000).

Saving the Little Bighorn Battlefield: *JIW* has previously noted the recent critical opportunities to preserve many key sections of the 1876 Little Bighorn Battlefield. The tracts include the site of Sitting Bull's village, all of the area of the river valley fight of Marcus Reno's command, and the routes used by the Northern Cheyenne and Oglalala Lakota warriots to attack George Custer's command on Custer Hill. The land is adjacent to Interstate 90 and U.S. Highway 212, making much of it suseptible to residential and commercial development. The owner of a partial interest in 120 acres of land has recently donated his interest to the Custer Battlefield Preservation Committee, giving that preservation organization the ability to prevent its spoilation. However, the group needs contributions to make payments on 1,000 or more acres it has optioned to purchase. *JIW* urges its readers to help whenever and however you are able. For information or to make contributions, contact Custer Battlefield Preservation Committee, P.O. Box 7, Hardin, MT 59034. (Source: James Court, Chairman).

Order of the Indian Wars Annual Assembly: The greatest Indian wars meeting of the latter part of 2000 will be held in Fort Collins, Colorado, August 24-27. The meeting will begin Thursday, the 24th, with a half-day of presentations on topics including the significance of the conflicts of the 1860s and the finding of the 1864 Sand Creek Massacre site. On Friday, conference participants will tour the 1868 Beecher's Island and 1869 Summit Springs Battlefields, the sites of key engagements in the wars for the southern Plains. On Saturday, the group will travel to Fort Laramie National Historic Site and the location of the 1854 "Grattan Massacre," the event which sparked two decades of war between the U.S. and the Sioux Indians. Saturday's tour will also include a visit to the little known site of the 1831 Battle of Natural Fort, where black frontiersman Jim Beckwourth led a Crow war party against a smaller group of Cheyenne. Saturday's tour will conclude with dinner at the Terry Bison Ranch and a banquet speech by novelist Terry Johnston.

The cost prior to July 27 is only $315 for Order of the Indians Wars members and $345 for non-members, a fee that includes the battlefield tours and most meals. An optional tour on Sunday ($65/$85) will include Rocky Mountain National Park and Buffalo Bill's grave on Lookout Mountain. For details and registration, write Order of the Indian Wars Assembly 2000, P.O. Box 7401, Little Rock, AR 72217, or e-mail aristotle.net. Tell them you saw this in *JIW*, and then join this worthwhile organization.

The Western History Association's 40th Annual Meeting will be held in San Antonio, Texas, October 11-14, 2000, at the Adam's Mark Hotel. Information may be obtained from Western History Association, University of New Mexico, 1080 Mesa Vista Hall, Albuquerque, NM 87131-1181. The meeting schedule may be found on the Internet at the association web site at www.unm.edu/~wha/index.html.

This year Adam Kane and Durwood Ball (University of New Mexico Press) are organizing what they hope will become a regular event at assocation meetings, a military scholar's luncheon. The intent is to produce a forum for meeting, discussing issues, and promoting scholarship in Western military history. This initial luncheon will be held at the Gunther Hotel and will focus on books and articles published within the past year. Adam Kane may be contacted at the address above by surface mail and at akane@unm.edu by e-mail.

Reenactment and Reconstruction: The Fort Buford [North Dakota] Sixth Infantry Regimental Association is one of the oldest Indian wars reenactment groups and is dedicated to presenting the life and schooling of infantry on the northern Plains. The group is currently beginning a reconstruction and restoration project at the site of Fort Buford, an important fort at the confluence of the Missouri and Yellowstone Rivers. To aid this project, the group is looking for photographs, diaries, journal, log books, and artifacts related to Fort Buford and specifically covering the years 1875-1881 at Fort Buford, the period of the infantry's occupation. If any readers can assist in this search, please contact Fort Buford Sixth Infantry Regimental Association, Box 159, Williston, ND 58802-0159. Web site: www.geocities.com/Athens/Oracle/6023. (Source: Richard K. Stengerb, Secretary).

NPS Battlefield Protection Program: The National Park Service's American Battlefield Protection Program extended through June a grant for a study and action plan by the Frontier Heritage Alliance for the locations of six engagements assocated with General George Crook and his Crow allies' 1876 campaigns against the Lakotas, Northern Cheyenne, and Northern Arapaho. The grant was the first ABPP grant given for the study of western Indian battles. The battle sites are those of the Rosebud, Powder River/Reynolds Battle, Sibley-Dull Knife Battle, Tongue River Heights, and Slim Buttes.

Crook's campaigns were part of what became known as the "Great Sioux War" and the Battle of Rosebud may well have affected the outcome of the better known Battle of the Little Bighorn. Project supervisor John D. McDermott identifies some of the project's ultimate goals as the preparation of a resource management plan for the Rosebud Battlefield State Park, development of the Indian side of the story, and the involvement of the Indian intellectual and collegiate community, bringing together of all interested parties in cooperative efforts, and making available information on the battle for planning and decision making.

The Frontier Heritage Alliance maintains an outstanding web site that contains news of this and other study preservation projects and also an extensive calendar of museum, tribe, and organization events on the northern Plains. The site URL is www.frontierheritage.org.

Book Review Editor: *Journal of the Indian Wars* is pleased to announce that Dr. Patrick J. Jung has joined our staff as book review editor. After earning an undergraduate degree in political science, Dr. Jung spent four years in the U.S. Army, including six months overseas in the Republic of Egypt, as an infantry officer and a paratrooper. He left the service in 1990 and began studies in American history at Marquette University, where he received his Master's in 1992 and his Ph.D. in 1997. He currently holds positions as an adjunct professor of history and as a prospect researcher in the Advancement Office at Marquette.

REVIEWS

Apache Nightmare: The Battle at Cibecue Creek, by Charles Collins (Norman: University of Oklahoma Press, 1999. Pp. Xvi, 280. Photographs, maps, notes, index. Cloth, $22.95)

On August 28, 1881, Colonel Eugene Asa Carr with two companies of his Sixth Cavalry and a company of White Mountain Apache scouts marched out of Fort Apache, Arizona Territory. Carr's orders from departmental commander General Orlando B. Willcox were to arrest a chief and spiritual leader of the Cibecue sub-tribal group of Western Apaches camped on Cibecue (Cibicu) Creek on the White Mountain portion of the San Carlos Reservation. The Apache's name was Nock-ay-det-klinne, and he claimed he could resurrect dead Indians once whites left the Apache lands. Nock-ay-det-klinne was holding trance-like spiritual dances to raise the dead at his Cibecue Creek encampment.

Although the arrest was successfully made, Carr's returning column was trailed by about sixty Cibecue Apaches. These warriors opened fire on the soldiers' camp at the end of the day. All but one of the Apache scouts defected and began shooting at the soldiers in what would be the only wholesale mutiny of Apache scouts in the history of the Indian wars. Nock-ay-det-klinne was killed in the action, as were seven troopers. The dead included a company commander, Captain Edmund C. Hentig.

For months, the Arizona Territory was in a state of panic as the rebellious area Apaches killed settlers and stole livestock in the White Mountains and even attacked Fort Apache. More troops were transferred into the affected territory. Eventually most of the belligerents surrendered. Several of the mutinous scouts were placed on trial, and three of them—Dead Shot, Dandy Jim, and Skippy—were hanged at Fort Grant in 1882. Their guilt in the affair remains problematic. Other deserters received prison terms.

Author Charles Collins convincingly argues that the Cibecue affair was a botched assignment by military authorities and that miscommunication, unfounded fears, and poor communication by the army interpreter Charles Hurrle led to the mutiny of the scouts. The author advances the argument that

Carr was looking for a fight when he left Fort Apache. Indeed the arrest may have been illegal, and no hard evidence exists that Nock-ay-det-klinne was inciting the Cibecue Indians to war. (During his interaction with the Cibecue Apaches during the early 1970s, this reviewer found they still had these long-held contentions.) Bickering in the high command, especially between Willcox and Carr—and eventually between Carr and Colonel Ranald S. Mackenzie—made matters worse and detracted from the reputation of success that Carr had established with the Republican River Expedition against the Dog Soldiers in 1869.

Collins' synthesis of the pertinent military records in the National Archives is exhaustive, and he presents the most complete analysis of the Cibecue incident written to date. As a product of such records, the book is heavily slanted toward the military point of view. The only Indian sources come from interviews by General George Crook with the Western Apaches following his reassignment to Arizona in 1882. Most of these Indians interviewed merely asserted their innocence; they did not attempt to illuminate the underlying causes and effects of the affair, especially in relation to the power and respect Nock-ay-det-klinne may or may not have possessed over other Apache groups. Collins apparently did not consult any of the modern Cibecue Apaches, some of who still hold strong beliefs and have passed down stories relating to this incident. The effects of the Battle of Cibecue remain uncertain, so that the Chiricahua Apache outbreak of the same year cannot be convincingly linked to the events at Cibecue Creek.

The spiritual movement of Nock-ay-det-klinne has, of course, long begged for comparative analyses with the Ghost Dance movement of the late 1880s among the Lakotas. Such comparison is not made in this work. No exhaustive comparative study of the Native American Messianic movements that emerged in response to the Indian Wars has yet been written. This lack of study of multi-ethnic world views has kept events like the Cibecue affair still shrouded in mystery.

John H. Monnett   Metropolitan State College of Denver

Little Bighorn Remembered: The Untold Indian Story of Custer's Last Stand, by Herman J. Viola, foreword by Gerard Baker. (New York: Times Book, division of Random House, 1999. Pp. Xiii, 240. Illustrations, maps, foreword, acknowledgements, contents, additional reading, contributors, index, cloth, $45.)

The Sacrificial Lion: George Armstrong Custer from American Hero to Media Villain, by Brice C. Custer, foreword by Gregory J. W. Urwin (El Segundo, CA: 1999. Order from Upton and Sons, Publishers, 917 Hillcrest Street, El Segundo, CA 90245; 1-800-959-1876. Volume XIII of the Montana and the West Series. Pp. Xiv, 293. Illustrations, maps, foreword, preface, notes, bibliography, index, cloth, $42.50.)

The victor in war typically writes the history of such conflicts. The accepted story of the Battle of the Little Bighorn is a case in point. In the standard interpretation, the Seventh Cavalry may have lost the battle, but the U.S. Army won the Great Sioux War of 1876-77 and forced the Lakota Sioux and their Northern Cheyenne allies onto the reservations. As Herman J. Viola notes, Custer's Last Stand "was also the last stand of the Sioux and Cheyenne as well, because their victory over Custer led to their own destruction." Ironically, in contributing to the defeat of the Sioux, the Crow and Arikara allies of the Seventh Cavalry failed to preserve their own traditional way of life. In the words of Gerard Baker, former Superintendent of the Little Bighorn Battlefield National Monument, the battle "was also a fight between the Indian tribes." The Crows' and Arikaras' participation in that conflict condemned them to share the same fate as the defeated "hostiles" who were confined to the reservation. None of the tribes, Viola contends, would "find any comfort in the events of 1876."

The historiography of the battle has traditionally reflected the perspective of the military at the expense of the Native American point of view. Viola's ambitious *Little Bighorn Remembered* is the latest effort in a long tradition of trying to present the Indians' side of the story. At the turn of the twentieth century, Indian Wars researcher Walter M. Camp interviewed several of Custer's Arikara and Crow scouts as well as Sioux and Cheyenne veterans of the battle. Camp's early death prevented him from realizing his goal of selecting from these accounts "such facts as seem incontrovertible and weave them with my own story. . . ." His exhaustive efforts went largely unnoticed until Kenneth

Hammer and Richard Hardorff published his research notes more than fifty years later.

Others successfully followed in Camp's footsteps. Among these pioneers was Orin G. Libby, whose *Arikara Narrative* appeared in 1920. Based on interviews with members of the Arikara tribe, Libby's seminal work presented the scouts' side of the story in their own words in a persuasive attempt to refute charges of cowardice among other misconceptions. In 1931, Dr. Thomas B. Marquis complemented Libby's valuable contribution with the publication of *A Warrior Who Fought Custer*, the recollections of Wooden Leg and other Northern Cheyenne warriors. A trusted friend and physician who was adept at sign language, Marquis wove this first person narrative into a coherent story of the journey of the tribe to the Little Bighorn and its aftermath. If Libby sought to dispel myths, Wooden Leg's story stimulated further controversy by its allusions to panic, intoxication, and suicide among Custer's troops.

In 1957, David Humphrey Miller's *Custer's Fall* actually focused on the role of the Sioux and Cheyenne at the expense of the military's point of view, if not historical accuracy. Fluent in the language of the northern Plains tribes, Miller based his account on the recollections of over seventy aged warriors who had been inhabitants of the great encampment on the Little Bighorn. He added fuel to the controversy over Marquis's conclusions by attributing the panic alleged by Marquis to Custer's death at the beginning of the fight.

What sets Viola's work apart is its successful attempt to depict the role of all four tribes who participated in the battle by drawing on a variety of sources and distinguished scholars. It complements the oral history compiled by Camp and others by focusing on the oral tradition preserved by the children and grandchildren of those who participated in the engagement that bloody June Sunday. The faithfulness of such tradition is apparent among the Cheyenne, who consistently attribute Custer's defeat to the false promise he made to their southern brethren when he induced them to surrender in 1869. "In Oklahoma, the Cheyenne made a peace pipe offering to Custer," recalled Charles Limpy, grandson of a Little Bighorn warrior. "Custer said he would never fight the Cheyenne again." In 1876, he broke that pledge.

Viola's synthesis will appeal to both the casual and the knowledgeable reader. The account of the Lakota chief Red Horse is a familiar one to every serious student of Custer's last battle. What enhances this printing is the color reproduction of the pictographic drawings that the chief drew when he was interviewed in 1881. The complete set has been published for the first time.

Depicting the battle in all its magnitude, the reader will readily agree that these graphic sketches from the National Anthropological Archives "combine a journalist's sense of story with the artist's eye for detail." The gruesome and depiction of Custer's dead realistically portrays an event often romanticized.

Little Bighorn Remembered thus adds something new to something old. New documentation confirms established facts (for example, the story of the Arikara scout Red Star). Yet this book also presents unknown details which will fascinate even the most serious Custer scholar. One such case may be found in the contribution by James S. Hutchins, which brings to light the papers of noted Western photographer Edward S. Curtis. Curtis in 1907 persuaded three of Custer's Crow scouts to reenact their participation in the events of June 25, 1876. What the scouts revealed in tracing Custer's final route to the battlefield dramatically reversed the traditional interpretation of the tactical reasons for his defeat. "The Crows' story," according to Hutchins, "turned all that upside down," implying Custer's abandonment of Reno's battalion. On the advice of President Theodore Roosevelt and others, Curtis did not publish this unbelievable story which would have further tarnished Custer's reputation.

To the Little Bighorn enthusiast, Herman J. Viola's book is not so much the untold but the overlooked story of Custer's last battle. Most of the contributions to this effort support this theme, including Douglas Scott's essay on archaeological findings; this new evidence complements the historical record of the victory of the Lakota and Cheyenne. However, some excellent essays which provide interesting new details and perspectives are not relevant to the purpose of this volume. Glenn Swanson's commentaries on Reno's retreat and Lieutenant William V.W. Reily's letters are a case in point. John Langellier's comprehensive essay on the transformation of George A. Custer from a mortal being to a mythical figure simply reinforces the traditional focus on that military leader at the expense of his Indian allies and opponents. It sheds no light on the other side of the story. Finally the pages devoted to Lakota oral tradition lack the substance and persuasion of their Cheyenne counterparts. Such shortcomings, however, are not critical. *Little Bighorn Remembered* is recommended to all who seek insights as to that fateful day in Montana in 1876.

The wise man soon learns that there are several sides to every story. If Herman J. Viola and others have portrayed the Indians' story of the Battle of the Little Bighorn, Brice C. Custer has presented his famous great-uncle's side of the story in *The Sacrificial Lion: George Armstrong Custer from American Hero to Media Villain*. Brice Custer is the first member of his family to come to

George Armstrong Custer's defense since the death of the colonel's widow in 1933. The author, as he admits, faces a difficult task given the negative image created by the media, notably in films such as *Little Big Man* and *Son of the Morning Star*. The very name Custer excites partisan emotions, and a book on the subject by a descendent should add fuel to the fire, if not generate skepticism. Although author Custer admits that he will not change the minds of the convinced Custerphobe, he hopes that his efforts will at least persuade the uninformed reader.

Long before Hollywood misrepresented Custer and his famous last battle, the "Boy General" of the Civil War had developed a reputation for reckless ambition. This reputation was further by his self-promotion in such writings as *My Life on the Plains*. The notoriety of Custer's ambition provided Custer's enemies with an easy explanation for what happened on that fateful day in 1876. In the wake of the battle, critics charged that the quest for glory led Custer to disobey Terry's written orders. In their view, Custer had prematurely attacked the Lakota Sioux and Northern Cheyenne encampment on the Little Bighorn before the scheduled arrival of Colonel John Gibbon's "Montana Column" on June 26, 1876. Major Marcus A. Reno, the senior surviving officer of the battle, alleged that Custer wanted "a big victory" over the Sioux before anyone else. "Custer was whipped," the major asserted, "because he was rash."

Reno had his own motivations for "trashing" Custer, but his blunt statement reflected wider criticism within the U.S. Army and anticipated the tone of the hostile press. Some of the denigration of Custer also came from those who sought to protect their own reputations by holding Custer responsible for the defeat of the Seventh U.S. Cavalry. General Alfred H. Terry, the expedition commander, blamed Custer for what he reputedly called a "sad and terrible blunder," "becoming the most prominent among those who kicked the dead lion in their own defense."

The hostility not only condemned Custer's role at the Little Bighorn, but cast a shadow over his entire military career. The reckless abandon he had demonstrated on the Civil War battlefields contained, in the eyes of many, the seeds of future disaster. Custer's last battle ensured legendary status while ironically demeaning his earlier accomplishments.

Brice Custer's defense of his ancestor reexamines key events in his great-uncle's career in order to neutralize the negative perception created by the disaster at Little Bighorn. The author thus examines Custer's Civil War record to document not only the general's undisputed courage and successes but also his sound judgment and selfless acknowledgement of the accomplishments of his subordinates in the Army of the Potomac. Brice Custer's analysis of the Washita Campaign of 1868-69 attempts not only to illustrate Custer's success as an Indian campaigner but also to repudiate misinformation about that battle that helped undermine the colonel's reputation. Most (including this reviewer) would agree with the author's observation that Custer's persuasion of the Cheyenne and Arapaho tribes to surrender peacefully after the Washita "was a major accomplishment during which Autie [Custer's family nickname] demonstrated considerable resourcefulness, determination and no small amount of courage." Because the discovery of gold paved the way for white settlement in the Dakotas, the 1874 Black Hills Expedition has further damaged Custer's reputation. But the author notes that it also negated the "false image" of Custer as an Indian killer when he spared the members of a small Sioux village from certain death at the hands of his scouts. If anything, Custer spoke out against the mistreatment of the red man.

Brice Custer's defense actually minimizes his great uncle's reputation as an Indian fighter. Although arguing that Custer was highly regarded as a campaigner on the Plains, the author notes that Custer had participated in only three Indian fights before the Little Bighorn, two of them merely skirmishes with the Lakota on the Yellowstone River in 1873. The author thus unwittingly recognizes one of the more important reasons for the Little Bighorn disaster—the inexperience of Custer's regiment. The Seventh Cavalry was far from being a battle-tested unit against the Plains Indians. This factor, coupled with the strength and determination of the tribes and the erroneous strategical assumptions of the military, better explains the outcome of Custer's Last Stand than speculation about the role of his subordinates and the impact of personality clashes.

George Armstrong Custer is not immune from criticism in this well written book. His descendant believes, for example, that his attempt to join his wife while on the dangerous campaign trail in 1867 "was the poorest judgment he ever exercised." The author concedes that Custer's preoccupation with preventing the escape of the Indian villagers at the Little Bighorn contained the seeds of defeat. Hindsight would demonstrate that "he should have been more concerned with the strength and temper of his opponents" in view of the warnings of his scouts.

Most scholars will agree with Brice Custer's sound analysis of the strategy of the Little Bighorn campaign. He correctly assumes that uncertainty about the location of the "hostile" encampment negates the accusation that Custer disobeyed orders by attacking a day before planned. As events demonstrated, the hostiles were not on the upper reaches of the Little Bighorn River or Rosebud Creek, as General Terry had assumed when he ordered Custer "in pursuit of the Indians." Brice Custer also correctly points out that the colonel's orders were discretionary, a flexibility made necessary by the acknowledged mobility of an elusive target. Finally, the author notes that if Custer was preoccupied with the flight of the Indians, it was a fixation he shared with the entire military chain of command.

For the less familiarized reader, *The Sacrificial Lion* provides an excellent, if partisan, overview of the Custer controversy. It is not a comprehensive biography of the man and his times, nor is it intended to be so. However, the serious student of Custer and his last battle will be disappointed, notwithstanding the cogent analysis. This reviewer expected that the book would produce a "smoking gun" to identify the "real culprit" at the Little Bighorn or at least present new details based on unpublished letters or other primary documents available to the Custer family. Yet the author candidly admits that the pages on the Little Bighorn contain no new information. With few exceptions, Brice Custer's endeavor is based on well-known secondary sources.

The Sacrificial Lion will not be the final word on the Custer controversy. Students of Custer and his last battle will continue to debate what happened on that day in Montana in 1876.

C. Lee Noyes   Morrisonville, New York

The Conquest of the Karankawas and Tonkawas, 1821-1859, by Kelly F. Himmel. (Texas A&M University Press, 1999. Pp. xvii, 192. Contents, preface, acknowledgements, appendices, notes, bibliography, index. Cloth, $32.95.)

Due to his interest in the sociological concept of "conquest," the historical period investigated by Kelly Himmel covers the years in which the most intense confrontations between the natives and newly arrived settlers in Texas took place. These violent encounters took place during the time that the former Spanish province of Tejas became a Mexican province, then became the Republic of Texas, and finally became a state integrated into the Union. The field of Native-American/Euro-American relations in Texas has been too long neglected in favor of more glamorized and easily researched areas. The interest of a sociologist such as Kelly Himmel in this forgotten part of American Indian history seems puzzling, but this in no way detracts from his accomplishment. In this laudable endeavor, Himmel brings together disparate historical sources to reconstruct the story of now-extinct Native American groups of the lower southern Plains and the coast of the Gulf of Mexico.

The cultural areas Himmel covers in this study have been grossly overlooked by academia. They have been often dismissed as a "cultural sink" where peoples without any historical relevance dwelt, peoples too marginal to compete with better known native groups at the frontier of European colonization. Apart from the Tonkawas, who now claim compensation for their losses, all the native groups he mentions in this historical sociology of the lower Plains have gone. The Cocos, Bidais, Karankawa, Lipan and Tawakonis, to cite just a few, have disappeared under the ravages of some of the most cruel and violent chapters in native peoples' history. An addition to the missing historical picture such as Himmel's *The Conquest of the Karankawas and Tonkawas* is a long overdue tribute to the history of these peoples and a memorial to their genocide.

Himmel carefully scrutinized original sources, including newspapers, travel notes, official speeches and reports. Though he points out the methodological and theoretical difficulty of reconstructing history only from the winners' side (we do not have any documents or oral histories of the natives), the author nevertheless offers to the readers a compelling and credible picture of Euro-American/American Indian interaction during the mid-nineteenth century. The difference between the attitudes of two of the area's most influential groups—the Karankawas and the Tonkawas—towards the settlers makes an interesting contrast. In addition, the two peoples' political decisions, strategic allegiances and cunning changes of flag, beyond describing differences in Native Americans' survival tactics, tell us the tragic story of disempowered groups fighting for their life during harsh times of change.

Throughout the book, the Anglo-American conquest of the southern Plains is viewed not just as a military effort to physically eliminate the native peoples living in the area, but rather as an orchestrated campaign that used media (newspapers, speeches) and religious, scientific and evolutionary discourses to further native peoples' extermination. This campaign included attacks on the Indians' reputation. Himmel makes the important point that condemnation of cultural elements specific to southern Plains Indians, such as ritual cannibalism, played a very significant role in the process of conquest. It is ironic then that the Tonkawas, the group most often accused of "eating their enemies," survived while the Karankawas, who were never known to practice anthropophagy ["man eating"], were destroyed by the accusation.

This irony and other interesting facets of southern Plains history have been highlighted by the painstaking work of a sociologist whose choice of topic fills a gap in Indian wars historiography. Kelly Himmel's effort to bring to scholarly attention this slice of Native American history is a good piece of academic work that surely will enrich our picture of past ethnic relations.

Massimiliano Carocci   Editor, *Anthropological Index Online*,
                              Royal Society of Anthropology of Britain and Ireland

Indian War Sites: A Guidebook to Battlefields, Monuments, and Memorials, by Steve Rajtar. (Jefferson, NC: McFarland & Company, Inc., 1999. Pp. 330. Preface, chronology, contents, bibliography, indexes. Cloth, $39.95, plus $4.00 shipping first book.) Order from McFarland & Company, Box 611, Jefferson NC 28640; 1-800-253-2187.

Indian War Sites is a unique reference work and resource. Hundreds of battles are described in thumbnail sketches, with their dates and at least approximate locations noted. A numbering system indicates which of the 425 works in the bibliography were the references for each entry. The book is very extensive, describing not only "Indian wars" battles but also encounters during European exploration, Civil War battles involving Indian troops, and violent incidents of the early twentieth century. In addition to events in the current United States, author Rajtar describes fifty-six engagements in Canada and Mexico.

However, there are several serious omissions from this work, notably every battle of the large-scale 1863-1864 campaigns against the Dakotas and Lakotas in present-day North Dakota. (This and other gaps might have been avoided had the author consulted *Indian Battles and Skirmishes on the American Frontier* or other reprints of the U.S. Army's battle chronologies.) There are also errors. The mistakes are most obvious when an entry is placed in the wrong state, as when Arizona's "Pima Uprising" is moved to New Mexico or when Colorado's Battle of Beecher Island and Oklahoma's Wichita Agency Fight are both relocated to Kansas. Separate incidents are sometimes treated as if they were a single event, as are the Meeker Massacre and the Thornburg Battle. A number of battles are placed in the wrong month or year. There are also occasional problems with the author's terminology. For example, Cochise's bloodless escape from captivity in the "Bascom Affair" is for some reason termed the "Battle at Siphon Canyon" (33); this word choice invites confusion with an intense armed engagement that later took place in the same area. Most of the errors are found in the coverage of Western events, the author doing a more accurate and thorough job when dealing with the colonial and early republican periods in the East.

Though promotional information says that "each entry has information about how to find the site" (www.amazon.com), *Indian War Sites* actually includes directions to only a fraction of the battlefields. The usefulness of the travel information is also uneven. For example, precise mileage is given to Kentucky's Fort Boonesborough State Park. However, under the entry for Idaho's Battle of White Bird Canyon (94-95), the author directs visitors to a fort site many miles away while failing to note that the battlefield itself may be toured as part of a national historical park. Similarly, while some information is very current, readers wishing to visit the site of the 1736 Battle of Ackia are misdirected to a park that lost its designation as "Ackia Battleground National Monument" (136) over thirty years ago when it was determined that the battle had taken place elsewhere.

Indian Wars Sites can serve as a "ready reference" in the form of an annotated chronology, index, and book list. For those using it for these purposes, the book may seem at times like an aged automobile—indispensable for transporting you while maddeningly in need of an overhaul.

Michael A. Hughes   Editor, *Journal of the Indian Wars*

BOOK NOTES

Because of the large number of Indian and military history books being published, *JIW* is unable to review all new titles in full. Our book notes section provides brief descriptions of older titles, reprints and revised editions, and important works not focused specifically on historic Indian conflicts.

The Dakota War: The United States Army Versus the Sioux, 1862-1865, by Micheal Clodfelter. (Jefferson, NC: McFarland & Company, Inc., 1998. Pp. 267. Illustrations, maps, contents, introduction, prologue, appendices, notes, bibliography, index. Cloth, $42.50, plus $4.00 shipping first book.) Order from McFarland & Company, Inc., Box 611, Jefferson NC 28640; 1-800-253-2187.

In a bibliographic essay in the last issue of *JIW*, the author stated that "there has been all too little published on the Sibley and Sully expeditions in present-day North Dakota." Happily, this shortage of material was addressed at book length two years ago with the publication of *The Dakota War*. In this well researched volume, author Micheal [sic] Clodfelter examines the causes, conduct, and consequences of warfare between the Dakota-speaking (i.e., "Sioux") nations and the U.S. from the Grattan Massacre of 1854 through the conclusion of the campaigns in present North Dakota in 1865. The book has some weaknesses. In particular, the ethnographic and linguistic information is sometimes confusing, and the description of the causes of the initial conflict in Minnesota is done in a cursory fashion.

At the same time, *The Dakota War* is wondrously comprehensive. Readers will here find material on such often overlooked events as the Spirit Lake Massacre, the "Battle of the Badlands," and the siege of Fort Dilts as well as the better known but still underexamined engagements of the Sibley and Sully campaigns. The author also makes a worthy contribution to Indian wars scholarship in his thoughtful analyses of the impact of the army campaigns, which he concludes encouraged rather than weakened long-term Indian resistance. *The Dakota War* belongs in any serious Western history collection, public or private.

Documents of American Indian Diplomacy: Treaties, Agreements, and Conventions, 1775-1979, 2 vols, by Vine Deloria, Jr., and Raymond J. DeMallie, with foreword by Daniel K. Inouye. (Norman: University of Oklahoma Press, 1999. Pp. 1539. Contents, foreword, introduction, bibliography, index. Cloth, $95.)

The five volume *Indian Affairs, Laws, and Treaties* (1903-1941), first edited by Charles Kappler, a clerk to the Committee on Indian Affairs, has long been the standard source of texts of published treaties between the United States and the Indian nations. However, Kappler's work has many shortcomings, including numerous omissions and misattached addenda. *Documents of American Indian Diplomacy* extensively supplements Kappler's volumes. *Documents* for the first time assembles the many important pacts made by the pre-Constitution Confederation government and by powers other than the United States, including foreign nations, the Confederacy, and the various individual states. Unratified treaties and agreements of the United States are also included. Such materials are very useful in studying competitive negotiation and the evolution of diplomacy in North America.

In addition, the easier access to original texts provided by *Documents* may help correct some common misconceptions. For example, the newly published materials reveal that Congress was often less malign in the amendment and ratification process than is generally assumed. (The authors believe that much of the mischief done to Indian treaties came through federal court interpretations rather than legislative action.) Scholars will also appreciate the chapters that explain how treaties were negotiated and how the original process of treaty negotiation came to an end. It must be noted, however, that despite the title few of the documents included in the volumes postdate 1900. If the work has one shortcoming, it is the inadequate index, which consists only of the names of Indian nations.

Documents of American Indian Diplomacy is an outstanding addition to the study of American Indian history and will be essential to any serious student of white–Indian conflict and compromise.

The Piikani Blackfeet: A Culture Under Siege, by John C. Jackson. (Missoula, MT: Mountain Press Publishing Company, 2000. Pp. 276. Illustrations, contents, preface, appendices, notes, bibliography, index. Paper, $18; cloth, $30.)

In *The Piikani Blackfeet* , independent scholar John C. Jackson examines the "Piikani" nation of the so-called Blackfeet confederacy in terms of its interaction with outsiders—whites in the form of fur and whiskey traders and missionaries, and other Indians in the form of allies and, much more commonly, enemies. With justification, he sees the "Piikani" as a people long besieged, threatened by dependence on trade, the impact of alcohol, and the loss of territory. Jackson does not ignore the long history of armed resistance by the much-feared Blackfoot nations. However, his discussion of the Blackfoot War, the height of conflict with the United States, is limited. Though he says of the 1870 Baker or Marias River massacre that this "most tragic of military actions against an unsuspecting community . . . has been largely overlooked" (note 337), he himself spends only three paragraphs on the event and cites only a single reference on the tragedy.

The author, though drawing on a wealth of secondary sources, drew on few primary sources concerning this or any other event. He apparently utilized almost no U.S. government documents, notably Superintendent of Indian Affairs and U.S. Army reports, and consulted few sources containing Blackfoot oral history. The latter omission may help explain why the author never notes that the Blackfeet peoples themselves use the spelling "Pikuni" versus "Piikani."

The *Piikani Blackfeet* is not a definitive work. However, it has the merits of being an affordable and very readable book and one of the only overviews of Pikuni/Piegan Blackfoot history.

Man Corn: Cannibalism and Violence in the Prehistoric American Southwest, by Christy G. Turner II and Jacqueline A. Turner (Salt Lake City: University of Utah Press, 1999.) Photographs, tables, contents, introduction, appendix, references cited, index, 547pp., cloth, $65.)

In an act of either courage or temerity, anthropologist Christy Turner, Jacqueline A. Turner, and the University of Utah Press have produced one of the most intriguing and controversial books in the history of American anthropology. The author's theses are deeply troubling to modern day descendants of the Ancestral Puebloans ("Anasazi") and to those sympathetic Euro-Americans who have maintained that Southwestern farming Indians have always lived in egalitarian and peaceful harmony. Turner maintains that systematic violence and cannibalism were practiced in the southwestern United States Four Corners area from the 900s through 1200s, that the atrocities were practiced as a form of social control by an elite, and that the practices were likely introduced directly from Mesoamerica. The authors reached these conclusions only after applying six separate forensic criteria to masses of skeletal remains, and the weight of the evidence presented on the butchering of ancient corpses is compelling.

However, the authors' suggestion of the arrival of an aggressive elite from the south is more difficult to defend. The architectural and iconographic clues that suggest Four Corners contact with Mexico remain problematic; many readers may also conclude that the authors make too much of isolated examples of dental evidence in arguing for a physical connection between the two regions. Still, this work is revolutionizing interpretations of the ancient Southwest. It furthers the conclusion that no human culture has ever been immune from the scourge of war.

Other Books Received

The following books have been received since the publication of *JIW* I-2 and are not yet reviewed, though they may be under consideration for review. The journal welcomes qualified book and video reviewers. If you are interested in writing reviews, please contact Dr. Patrick Jung, *JIW* Book Review Editor, 2915 N. 84th Street, Milwaukee, WI 53222; e-mail address: patrick.jung@marquette.edu. Please include information on your qualifications, your areas of interest, and any specific titles or types of works in which you have an interest. Information on our format for reviews may be found on the www.savaspublishing.com web site via the *Journal of the Indian Wars* page, or obtained by writing or e-mailing Dr. Jung.

The Fox and the Whirlwind: General George Crook and Geronimo, A Paired Biography, by Peter Aleshire (John Wiley & Sons, 2000) [being reviewed].

Sagwitch: Shoshone Chieftain, Mormon Elder, 1822-1887 , by Scott R. Christensen (Utah State University Press, 1999).

Exploration of Ancient Key-Dweller Remains on the Gulf Coast of Florida , by Frank Hamilton Cushing (University Press of Florida, 1897; reprint 2000).

Playing Indian, by Philip J. Deloria (Yale University Press, 1999).

King Philip's War: Civil War in New England, 1675-1676, by James D. Drake (University of Massachusetts Press, 2000).

Mountain Scouting, a Handbook for Officers and Soldiers on the Frontier, by Edward S. Farrow (University of Oklahoma Press, 1881; reprint 2000).

The Iroquois in the Civil War, by Laurence M. Hauptman (Syracuse University Press, paper printing 1999) [being reviewed].

Contemplations of a Primal Mind, by Gabriel Horn (University Press of Florida, 1996, 2000).

Phil Sheridan and His Army, by Paul Andrew Hutton with foreword by Robert M. Utley (University of Oklahoma Press, paper printing 1999) [being reviewed].

Little Bighorn (Battlefields Across America series [juvenile]), by Randy Krehbiel (Twenty-First Century Books, 1997)

Pioneer Days in the Black Hills: Accurate History and Facts Related by One of the Early Day Pioneers, by John S. McClintock, edited by Edward L. Senn, foreword by Jerome A. Greene (University of Oklahoma Press, 2000).

Apache, & Comanche Military Societies, by William C. Meadows (University of Texas Press, 1999) [being reviewed].

Exploration of the Etowah Site in Georgia, ed. by Warren King Moorehead (University Press of Florida, 1932; reprint 2000).

North American Indian Wars (Turning Points in World History series), edited by Don Nardo (Greenhaven Press, 1999).

The First Global War: Britain, France, and the Fate of North America, 1756-1775, by William R. Nester (Praeger, 2000) [being reviewed].

Indians in the United States and Canada, by Roger L. Nichols (University of Nebraska Press, 1998) [cloth edition previously reviewed in Book Notes].

The Ute Indians of Utah, Colorado, and New Mexico, by Virginia McConnell Simmons (University Press of Colorado, 2000) [being reviewed].

To Hell with Honor: Custer and the Little Bighorn, by Larry Sklenar (University of Oklahoma Press, 2000 [being reviewed].

Borderlander: The Life of James Kirker, 1793-1852, by Ralph Adam Smith (University of Oklahoma Press, 1999).

People of the Wind River: The Eastern Shoshones, 1825-1900 , by Henry E. Stamm, IV (University of Oklahoma Press, 1999).

European and Native American Warfare, 1675-1815, by Armstrong Starkey (University of Oklahoma Press, paper printing 1998) [being reviewed].

Indian War in the Pacific Northwest: The Journal of Lieutenant Lawrence Kip, with introduction by Clifford E. Trafzer (University of Nebraska Press, introduction 1999).

Atlas of the North American Indian, rev. ed., by Carl Walden (Checkmark Books, 2000).

The Guns That Won the West: Firearms on the American Frontier, 1848-1898, by John Walter (Greenhill Books, 1999).

RESPONSE TO REVIEW

Author John D. McDermott, who wrote *A Guide to the Indian Wars of the West*, took issue with several observations in the review of his book in *JIW* I, 2. In fairness to Mr. McDermott, we will publish two points that he raised. First, he explains that cuts in his footnotes obscured the extent to which he presented new research, and second, that he was one of seven researchers who authored the National Park Service's *Soldier and Brave*, which the review correctly identified as the source from which he derived much travel information. We should note that *JIW* 's evaluation of McDermott's *A Guide to the Indian Wars of the West* was largely positive. In fact, despite the review's describing some specific problems with the travel section of the work, we recommended the book's historical section as a handy and useful reference in our online author guidelines.

We thank John McDermott, and all of our readers, for taking the time to write, and we appreciate your enthusiastic support of *JIW*.

INDEX

New and Forthcoming Titles!

The Wagon Box Fight:
An Episode of Red Cloud's War,
by Jerry Keenan

One of the best known Indian battles of the post Civil War West, the Wagon Box Fight has long attracted the interest of writers and students of the Indian Wars. This engagement, in which thirty-two defenders, armed with a newly arrived breech-loading rifle, held off scores of Indian attackers, was the army's response to the tragic Fetterman disaster. Keenan, an Indian Wars expert, has completely revised this edition to include an introduction to the development of the Bozeman Trail, the creation of Fort Phil Kearny, and the events leading up to the Wagon Box Fight. Also included are appendices containing official army reports of the principal officers, as well as a section on the archaeological field work at the site completed by the state of Wyoming. ISBN: 1-882810-87-2 ; three maps, 27 photos and illus. 12 charts, 168pp. $14.95. Release date: October 2000.

Expanded and Revised!

Triumph & Defeat:
The Vicksburg Campaign
By Terrence J. Winschel

Recipient of the 1999 Eastern National Author's Award!

"If *Triumph & Defeat* had been on the shelves of the Park library in September 1955, when I first entered on duty at Vicksburg, it would have provided the missing one volume introduction to the campaign and siege that I craved."

- Historian Edwin C. Bearss

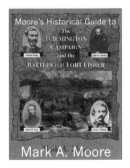

Moore's Historical Guide to the Wilmington Campaign and the Battles for Fort Fisher
By Mark A. Moore

The penultimate map / history of this important campaign! This study is enhanced with dozens of original maps on all the battles for Wilmington, including the battles for Fort Fisher. Moore's book includes explanatory notes, quotes from participants, orders of battle, scores of photos, and other graphics. Also includes detailed discussion of Crimean War similarities. Foreword by Chris E. Fonvielle. 8 ½ x 11, maps, photos, index, 222pp. Paper only. ISBN 1-882810-19-8. $15.95

· Available at fine bookstores everywhere ·

Savas Publishing Company

202 First Street SE, Suite 103A, Mason City, IA 50401; 515-421-7135 (phone); 515-421-8370 (fax); cwbooks@mach3ww.com (e-mail); www.savaspublishing.com (website)

The Western Historical Quarterly

The official journal of the Western History Association presenting articles dealing with the North American West.

AVAILABLE ON MICROFILM

Volumes 1 - 28 (1970-1997)
One volume per reel.
1 - 4 reels = $25 per reel
5 or more reels = $20 per reel

RESTOCK SINGLE ISSUES

Take a moment and restock your
WESTERN HISTORICAL QUARTERLY shelves:

All issues available except
Volume X, No. 1 (January 1979), Volume XII, No. 3 (July 1981), all of Volume XXII (1990)

$10.00 a single issue
Reprints may also be available of articles, $4.00
Accumulative Article Index, $30.00

TO PLACE YOUR ORDER:

Send check or money order to:

WESTERN HISTORICAL QUARTERLY
Utah State University
Logan UT 84322-0740

Cost of shipping will be billed separately.
For questions, Tel: 435-797-1301
Email: bstewart@hass.usu.edu

The Journal of Military History

a quarterly publication of the
Society for Military History

Essays on every aspect of the history of ground,
naval, and air forces and their
impact on society

Review essays   Articles in other periodicals
Historiographic essays   Annual dissertations list
Book Reviews   Annual index

Cumulative Index, 1937–1994, available

Quarterly since 1937: January, April, July, October

Individual memberships: US$35.00
Institutional subscriptions: US$55.00

Additional postage outside Canada-US-Mexico
$8.00 surface; $40.00 air (payable in US funds only)

Subscribe via the internet at www.smh-hq.org

For a free sample copy, to subscribe, or to submit an essay write:

Journal of Military History
George C. Marshall Library
Dept. I
Lexington, Virginia 24450–1600

Some recent essays:

"Raiding Strategy: As Applied by the Western Confederate Cavalry in the
American Civil War," Christopher S. Dwyer

"U.S. Navy Radio Intelligence During the Second World War and the Sink-
ing of the Japanese Submarine I-52," Carl Boyd

"Drill, Training, and the Combat Performace of the Civil War Soldier: Dis-
pelling the Myth of the Poor Soldier, Great Fighter," Mark A. Weitz

"Unexplored Questions about the German Military During World War II,"
Gerhard L. Weinberg

"Preserving the 'Habits and Usages of War': William Tecumseh Sherman,
Professional Reform, and the U.S. Army Officer Corps, 1865–1881,"
Mark R. Grandstaff

"Measuring the Political Articulateness of United States Civil War Soldiers:
The Wisconsin Militia," Joseph Allan Frank

"The Sexual Behavior of American GIs During the Early Years of the Occupation of Germany," by John Willoughby

Jerry L. Russell, Founder and National Chairman

THE STUDY OF THE MILITARY HISTORY of the early settlement of North America, and the continuing conflicts between Indian and Indian, Indian and settler, Indian and soldier, has long been a subject that has fascinated succeeding generations of Americans.

In the early decades of this century, an organization known as **The Order of Indian Wars of the United States**, made up primarily of retired military men, actual veterans of the Indian Wars, devoted its attention to the study of the U.S. military establishment's role in the development and settlement of this country's westward-moving frontier. That organization became an affiliate of the American Military Institute in 1947, and is once again active for descendants.

IN 1979, WE FOUNDED A **NEW** ORGANIZATION, inspired by that other group--a "spiritual descendant," if you will--but having no connection, official or otherwise with the predecessor. Our purpose, however, is similar--but broader: the in-depth study and dissemination of information on America's frontier conflicts. We are as interested in the "Indian side" as in the "Army/settlers side," although this organization, and its Assemblies, are not to be a forum for political or sociological crusades or guilt trips---our interest is in **military history**.

An additional purpose, equally important, we believe, is our concern for the historic preservation of those important sites associated with the history of the Indian Wars in America.   Citizens' groups **must** become more involved in historic preservation, or much of our past will be irretrievably lost, in the name of 'progress'. Historic military sites are an important part of our national heritage, and the preservation/protection of these sites will be a major, continuing, concern of our organization--hence our motto: WE WHO STUDY MUST ALSO STRIVE TO SAVE! HERITAGEPAC is the national lobbying organization established in 1989 to work for preservation of battlesites. Our main publication is the *OIW Communique*.

DUES ARE $20 A YEAR.

Our 21st Annual National Assembly, Focusing on the 125th Anniversary of The Red River War, will be held September 16-18, 1999, in Amarillo, Texas, With Tours Led By Neil C. Mangum, Superintendent, Little Bighorn Battlefield, to Adobe Walls, Palo Duro Canyon & The Washita Battlefield, Plus 12 Speakers.

WRITE FOR INFORMATION.
Order of the Indian Wars
P. O. Box 7401, Little Rock AR 72217

501-225-3996   > indianwars@aristotle.net <

The Writings of

JAMES WILLERT

Pertaining to the Battle of the Little Big Horn

Little Big Horn Diary. Updated new edition of the most detailed and comprehensive work ever done on the Battle of the Little Big Horn. Covers the summer campaign from May 17, 1876, to the rescue of Reno's men following the battle. The daily movements of all the units in the field are followed until the climax at LBH. Willert has added a supplement in addition to a 3,000 word essay that does not appear in the first printing of 20 years ago, making this a "must have" book even for owners of the rare first edition. *Custer Trail Series*, *Volume Six*. 480 pages, drawings, photos, biblio., Index. ISBN 0-912783-27-3. $125.00

> "The most comprehensive factual assemblage of the LBH data ever produced."
> *Robert Utley*

> "The finest work on Custer I have ever read."
> *Michael Koury*

March of the Columns: Chronicle of the 1876 Indian War. The sequel to *Little Big Horn Diary*. Begins where *LBHD* leaves off, on June 27, 1876, and follows the units all the way through the summer campaign until September 16, 1876. Commences with the rescue of Reno's command on the bluffs overlooking the LBH River. Contains substantial information on the aftermath of the Custer battle, as told by survivors. *Custer Trail Series*, *Volume Four*. 643 pages, 300,000 words, ISBN 0-912783-23-0. $85.00

> "Together, Jim Willert's two volumes ... Are an indispensable work to any serious student of the Sioux Campaign of 1876.."
> *Robert Utley*

To the Edge of Darkness. General Gibbon's Montana Column and The Reno Scout, March 4 - June 20, 1876. Examines in detail the daily happenings and adventures of the Montana Column and the controversial Reno Scout. This is the third volume of the lifelong work of James Willert, the other two being *Little Big Horn Diary*, and *March of the Columns. Custer Trail Series*, *Volume Seven*. 224 pages, 59 Van Ess illustrations and sketches, 8 maps plus end papers. 8 ½ x 11 red linen binding with gold stamping. ISBN 0-912783-28-1. $90.00

Special Willert Trilogy Discount Offer:
This outstanding set retails for $300. Purchase all three
James Willert books and save 20% ($60). Your price: only $240

UPTON AND SONS, PUBLISHERS
917 Hillcrest Street, El Segundo, California 90245
Web Site: www.uptonbooks.com / E-Mail: richardupton@worldnet.att.net
FREE CATALOG / ORDER: 800-959-1876 / Fax: 310-322-4739